About the Author

Raised in a small seaside town in County Dublin, Ireland. The author has lived there most of her life and raised a family. Growing up, she was told stories about how they got their last name but there was little evidence to back it up. After losing her father in 2018, she set out to see if these stories were true. The journey she was on was emotional and fascinating. It finally ended a chapter in her life when she found out where she was from and who had gone before her. She was determined to tell their story.

Le Petit: A Life Remembered

Maureen Petson

Le Petit: A Life Remembered

Olympia Publishers
London

www.olympiapublishers.com
OLYMPIA PAPERBACK EDITION

Copyright ©Maureen Petson 2023

The right of Maureen Petson to be identified as author of
this work has been asserted in accordance with sections 77 and 78 of
the Copyright, Designs and Patents Act 1988.

All Rights Reserved

No reproduction, copy or transmission of this publication
maybe made without written permission.
No paragraph of this publication may be reproduced,
copied or transmitted save with the written permission of the publisher,
or in accordance with the provisions
of the Copyright Act 1956 (as amended).

Any person who commits any unauthorised act in relation to
this publication may be liable to criminal
prosecution and civil claims for damage.

A CIP catalogue record for this title is
available from the British Library.

ISBN: 978-1-80074-970-2

This is a work of creative nonfiction. The events are portrayed to the
best of the author's memory. While all the stories in this book are true,
some names and identifying details have been changed to protect the
privacy of the people involved.

First Published in 2023

Olympia Publishers
Tallis House
2 Tallis Street
London
EC4Y 0AB

Printed in Great Britain

Dedication

Dedicated to my wonderful father whom I miss very much.
"I found him, Daddy."

Acknowledgements

I can't thank enough my beautiful daughter Sophie for her support and patience, when I went on and on about the discoveries I was making. "I love you to the moon and back."

My wonderful and caring friend Sylvia who pushed me to be my best self and never stopped believing in me. "You are amazing."

And finally, my lovely neighbour Martin who told me my book was great, at a time I was ready to give up. He gave me the confidence to continue. "So, thank you so much."

Foreword

When we set out to research our ancestors, we must be kind, for when we look back; we must try and put ourselves in that decade. The strength and mental ability needed to survive in this period is incomprehensible to us in this modern age.
We in this modern world have the privilege of saying 'No!'

We have the privilege to shape our own destiny and the means to do it.

We have the privilege to stand up or stand down, with little consequence.

We can be an individual or run with the crowd.

They had no such privileges. Punished for being poor, no right to an education, poor living conditions, no access to medical care, dying of diseases we take for granted. Controlled by the teachings of the Catholic Church, Even a burial within the city of Dublin (if you were Catholic) was denied to them for decades.

Surviving was a privilege.

If you read certain parts and feel offended, put yourself in their shoes, for when you have nothing, and God places a gift before you, there for the taking, you will grab it! Don't feel sorry for your ancestors for amid the harshness and the darkness there was also joy and camaraderie.

So be kind to their memory when you view their lives, because of them and their suffering and sacrifices we are now free to be privileged.

Because of John Le Petit, there was I,. Maureen Petson.

Introduction

Dublin during the 1800s had been the height of colonial fashion; even better than London with its lords, dukes and duchesses, its viscounts, countesses and peers of the realm. It was the place to be.

Leaving their country estates and their troublesome tenants, they would flock to Dublin and their City mansions for the winter. This was the season for balls, operas and theatres and the never-ending social gatherings. This in turn supplied the people of Dublin City with work from the carpenter to the baker, from the coal merchant to the servant. All trades plied their wares. Aristocrats lived comfortably and the world turned according to their tune.

But for the Irish Catholic population, one season was much like the next, the endless toll of trying to survive. They were the invisible mass, the cog in the wheel of industry, kept poor and ignorant. They were of little significance to their indifferent masters.

Many things would change in the beginning to the middle of the 1800s. Life for the poor of Ireland would take a drastic spiral downwards. As if it was possible to get any worse, it surely would, and did.

The act of Union 1801, Abolishing Parliament in Dublin and centralising government in London would cause a domino effect. The wealthy, all depending on parliament for their living and status, packed up and left for London, taking most of the commerce with them and reducing the most vulnerable and oppressed to absolute squalor.

Later, with the poor already living a precarious existence, the fatal potato famine 1845–1849 would cause over a million Irish people to starve to death, while the British government stood idly by. Another two million, oppressed, starving and diseased, fled Ireland's shores, never to return. One out of seven wouldn't survive the journey to that better land. Others over time would leave their mark so indelibly in their new country that the island of Ireland would stand up to be counted as a player on the international stage. A small nation, but a significant one!

The Irish are a resilient lot. Quick to adapt. Quick to laugh. Quick to sing and drink themselves happy. While everyone was in the same boat, they would stick together against the common enemy. They would hold each other up and help each other out, when circumstances allowed. Family was the key to living or dying; without that helping hand, you were lost, or destined for the workhouse.

Life was as fragile as a feather in a storm.

The unrest in Ireland would slowly grow. All the injustices would become too hard to bear. To be an Irish Catholic meant you were subject to poor living and working conditions: no education; no workers' rights; no access to medical care; even a burial within the city of Dublin was denied to them. About a third of the population still spoke Irish as their first and only language. There was little or no chance to improve one's lot, just one continual vicious circle of work, eat, and repeat.

Over the centuries, a few would stand up for change and would be quickly cut down by the British Establishment. In time, however, the voices of the Irish people would be heard and their determination to make a better job of governing themselves would urge them to fight for their freedom. They kept trying until they finally won.

Tiocfaidha'r la' (our day will come) became their anthem.

But, in 1861, life was still a hard every day battle. A struggle for survival and this is where my story begins.

Beresford Street, Dublin, 1861

In 1861, Dublin was alive and colourful with a swelling population of four hundred thousand people. Dublin incorporated the fruit and vegetable markets of Capel Street. The hustle and bustle of the fish markets at Smithfield. The perpetual smell of Jameson's Brewery, all mixed with the noise of Dublin docks, echoing up the river Liffey. This was home to three quarters of a million people.

The Douglas family had come from Co Meath, after the famine, in search of work. After losing his wife and one of his children from smallpox, Edward Douglas had made the decision to move his remaining daughter Maryanne and his two sons James and Patrick to live in Dublin City. Supported by a tightly knit community of neighbours, 61 Beresford Street was home. It resided in a tight cobbled lane of three-storey tenement houses, packed from attic to cellar with families. The house was divided into rooms, which families rented within the tenement house. They lived and worked here, as there were all kinds of industry from Jameson Malt Store to the thriving docks.

The roars and yelling of haggling resounding from every corner of the very busy markets made this area a hive of activity that boasted trades from carpenters to coal merchants, cabinetmakers to bricklayers, goldsmiths to jewellers, dairymaids to servants, and of course labourers. Eddie (as he was known), a short stocky man with a handlebar moustache, was a paviour. A trade passed down from father to son; the wealthy liked their carriageways to be formal and stylish. They employed paviours to decorate their entrance halls and create paths to guide the eye around their decorative gardens, and this Eddie did with great skill. So the family never starved and were a little better off than many others. Life revolved around getting work and keeping the family fed, with a roof over their heads.

With Mary's mother gone, it was down to her to do the hard and endless work of caring for her two brothers and her father Eddie. But when you know nothing else, this seems the norm. Lots of families lost mothers in childbirth or illness and the next female in line had to take up the slack; otherwise, families would be split up and be lost forever. Mary was content to carry out her daily tasks; washing, cooking, and bringing up water from the backyard. Cooking and cleaning were just part of her day.

It was also every woman's job to keep the stairwell and landing outside their doors scrubbed and clean. Mary would dutifully join her neighbour every day, bucket and scrubbing brush in hand to clean her share of the stairs and landing. It was the men's job to wipe their boots before entering the house or bear the wrath of all the women of the tenement. Many a poor soul had gone running as a hail of curses were heaped upon him for forgetting this rule.

Mary had not gone to school or played in the streets with the other chislers[1]. Now seventeen, she was a woman, or to some considered a spinster, left on the shelf.

Eddie was a decent sort of chap; he loved his family and he worked hard to give his sons the skills as a paviour, in the hope they would always find work. It had not gone unnoticed by Eddie just how hard life was for his daughter. He often watched her in the light of the tallow candles tending the fire or mending a shirt.

---

[1]Chislers: children

A sense of pride would well up inside his chest. How well she had coped after her mother's death. He noticed how pretty she had become, more and more like her blessed mother. "God be good to her." Mary was just a little slip of a girl, standing just five foot. She was known to have a pleasant nature and was often heard humming as she went about her chores. He always made one of the lads bring up the coal from the cellar so she didn't have to carry it up all those flights of stairs and sometimes the water too.

Mary would always smile. "Ah sure, Da, I don't mind getting da water, it gives me a chance to get all the gossip from tother women." She would give a little laugh and hug her da tightly, grateful that he had thought of her.

"Go way outtadat, would ye," Eddie would reply, embarrassed by the show of affection but secretly pleased.

He reminded himself to tell the lads to get her a little something, maybe some shoes from the second-hand trader in the market. He had noticed of late she was going barefoot. *No daughter of his would go barefoot,* he had vowed to himself. He would remember to tell the boys to pick her up something when they got their wages. *Can't have them taking her for granted,* or they would do the same to their wives when the time came and that might not be long from now, for he had noticed a wee lass Catherine from the lane making eyes at young Pat, as they set off for work each morning.

"Howa, Pat," she'd call as she hung the wash in the lane, swishing her skirt and lowering her head with a smile. Pat would tip his cap and go red, putting his head down, hoping his da hadn't heard. But Eddie would laugh to himself and just pat his son's back and move him on.

"Work to be done, lad, go on now, plenty of time for da ladies later." He'd wink at his son, making him go redder.

Now Mary had her own cap set on someone. She had known him most of her life and never noticed how handsome he was until lately. He was tall, (well to her five feet,) and dark, not like the other boys around here. Of course, she'd never let him see her watching him. She'd die! But watch him, she did.

His skin was sallow and his eyes oh! His eyes were like black coals with eyelashes that fanned his rosy cheeks. *Any woman would kill for lashes like that,* she'd often thought. He was slender, but so were all the boys; food wasn't something plentiful around here. Still you could see his young body starting to develop. Shoulders restless to broaden, Muscles straining in his thick wool shirt. When he lifted his woollen cap to say, "Grand day", in a soft voice and a shy smile, a mop of black curly hair fell around his face. Mary had blushed a little as she thought about him. Yes! He was for sure a handsome one, that John Le Petit.

The French's hatred for the British was as bitter as that of the Irish, making them the perfect allies. They had sent help in the shape of fleets of ships carrying guns and men during the failed 1798 rising in Ireland, and countless other times too, in the hope of banishing the English from Ireland forever. They would then join forces with the Irish, to rid themselves of the English in their own land.

Because of this, there had always been migration back and forth between the two nations. For John Le Petit Snr, it was a simple choice to flee France at a time of great unrest and poverty in his own country and take his young wife and start anew in Ireland. They had landed in Queenstown[2] in 1847 and tried

---

2. Queenstown: city now known as Cork

working a small plot of land for a few years. But his decision to migrate to Ireland at that time had landed them right in the middle of the Irish famine. So when his wife died from typhus, he took his young son, John, in search of work to Dublin and had lived in Mary's Lane ever since.

"I think his name sounds exotic: Le Petit or Petty or whatever it is, like he's from some exotic foreign land," Mary giggled to Catherine, her friend from the lane.

They were doing the laundry and they rubbed and scrubbed and dreamed.

"But, Mary, he's not really Irish now, is he? He's a blow in, that's what me Da says. In any ways, why would ye want that?" Pondered Catherine. "Not like your Pat, now there's a real Irish man," she said wistfully.

Mary had slapped her washing down hard, sending water splashing over Catherine. She glared at her friend who stood spluttering, covered in suds. Catherine realised she had said the wrong thing, and tried to back track. Wiping her face with her apron, she cautiously proceeded. "Sure, he's only gorgeous, so he is," she reassured her friend. "Truly, Mary, he is," she said, nodding at Mary. "It's just that your Pat's more my sort of man. 'Ere would ya put in a word with Pat for me?" She'd nudged her friend and splashed her a little with the soapy water.

Mary came round and giggled; of course, she'd put a word in for her friend with her favourite brother. 'Ere wait till I show ya d' petticoat, Pat got me at the clothes stall," Mary said reaching into her basket. She pulled out a second-hand petticoat; it had a few tears here and there, but Mary would mend that, no problem. The material was of good cotton and it had layers of frills starting midway and carrying on right to the bottom.

"Oh! Ye lucky cow." Catherine gasped. "I'm so jealous. 'Ere

d'ya think Pat will gets me one?" she said hopefully.

"Sure, he doesn't even know you're alive," Mary had snapped a little too abruptly.

Catherine had put her head down, hurt by Mary's harshness. Ignoring her and bringing the conversation back to the petticoat, Mary continued, "I'm going to dye it red. I got some ruam[3] in the market; ye has to seal it by soaking it in stale piss, ya know? Sure! Won't I be grand?" Mary explained as she held it up proudly.

"You surely will, Mary," answered Catherine enviously, as she stood back and admired the petticoat. "But sure y has rinse it well or ya surely will be grand! Grand and pissy." She laughed at her own joke and they continued their washing in silence. Mary thought of John as she scrubbed away at the dirty clothes, that John Le Petit was some fine chap. He truly was and she planned to have him, sure wouldn't every girl in the lane be mad with jealousy. Yes, he would be hers!

Little did Mary know, but John had spotted her too. She was different from the other girls. She had a spark in her. A fire burned in her eyes and he liked the way she stood up for herself, not running to her brothers for help. No, not her: she'd stand with one hand on her small waist and tilt her head and take on anyone. He liked that. God help the fool who tried to mess with that feisty miss. Her smile was broad and welcoming, and he loved her long wavy brown hair that she tied up with a ribbon. He imagined untying that ribbon, smelling her hair and looking into her hazel eyes. He dreamed of lifting her up, so her pink lips were close to his and gently kissing her.

But sure he hadn't even spoken to her, so how the hell that was going to happen, he couldn't figure out. Every bloody time

---

[3]Ruam: bark of the Ruam tree used to dye clothes, sometimes The Adler Tree was used.

he saw her, he was covered in coal dust from lifting the coal down the chutes at the big houses; at times, his eyes would be red and swollen from the rising dust. There had been a few stolen glances and lingering looks and he'd tried at times to chat to her. But she would be giggling and chatting with her friends. So he would just go on his way. *Face it, John, you've more chance of having pigs fly outa your ass then getting close to her,* he had scolded himself.

He didn't really have many friends, so he had no one to confide in, and no idea how to go about getting Mary's attention; he had felt very much of an outsider, as if he didn't fit in. Not having an Irish name or looking practically Irish made him stand out more than most. But things were better than they had been two years ago. Then fate stepped in to lend a helping hand.

Tom O'Grady was a local thug, whose long greasy hair clung to his face. Broken yellowing teeth appeared when he gave his menacing grin. He reeked of stale sweat and alcohol and his raggy clothes hung lifeless and soiled on his huge frame. He was known to all the women of the lane, which made sure never to be out alone after dark. They thought he was a bit touched in the head, and feared him, as he was known to leer at them, licking his lips. But he was far from touched in the head, he was just a bad egg, and you could be sure he was always out to do wrong.

One evening in late autumn, John found himself returning home after his week's work, wages safely tucked in his waistcoat pocket. He made his way through the narrow, cobbled streets towards Mary's Lane. At one of the particularly darker part of the lane, just waiting at the top, stood a tall, rather stocky figure, standing legs apart, fist clenched, half in shadow half in light, silhouetted by the lamp light.

As John drew closer, he realised it was O'Grady and he became a little nervous. O'Grady's reputation for being violent was well-known. His stomach churned in anticipation as he carried on up the lane. As he drew closer, he caught the menacing grin on O'Grady's face. "Give us da money, boy," he snarled.

"Feck off," John replied, trying to sound brave, as he pushed past him. As quick as a flash, O'Grady pounced on John and began pounding his large fists into his face and body. John tried to fight back, but O'Grady was twice his size. O'Grady's massive fists kept pounding and pounding until John lost consciousness. When he awoke he was bloodied and bruised; the pocket of his waistcoat had been ripped off and its contents long gone.

Word of the attack spread through the lanes. This was breaking a code that every man lived by here: 'No working man was ever to be interfered with'. People were disgusted by what had happened.

About a week later, John was sitting with his father by the fire in their small room, his bruises starting to fade. They noticed a piece of newspaper being pushed under the door. Surprised, John rose to retrieve it and stood gasping at the contents. Wrapped up in the newspaper was the majority of his wages. He quickly pulled the door open. But no one was there.

He stared at his papa. "What's dis, Papa?" a bewildered John asked, showing him the money.

"Justice, mon fils." (Justice, my son) His father had solemnly nodded in reply. John never knew just how he'd gotten his wages back. But he did notice that now O'Grady walked with a heavy limp. Much to John's relief, O'Grady soon left the area. But he would always remember O'Grady, thanks to a small scar he now carried on his left cheek.

From then on, John seemed to blend in better with the other men and made some lasting friendships. As was the custom of the

Irish, to call each other by their last names, the men of the lane had decided to call John 'Murray'. Le Petit , just didn't roll off the tongue that easily. So he became known as Murray, not that John cared what they called him as long as he fitted in.

"Come on, lad, less daydreaming, gets to work. I need these bags lifted on the cart now!" screeched Mr Walsh the coal merchant ,jolting him from his memories. He couldn't lose this job. The pay was decent and it helped keep him and his papa from starving. So John tipped his cap and worked on, leaving his dreaming till bedtime.

Now as luck would have it, Mrs Carey was very fond of a get together and any occasion would do. This occasion was a farewell to her eldest daughter and son-in-law who would be leaving Ireland to take their chances in the Americas. They were due to set sail from Queenstown[4]. It had cost them seven pounds sterling each for their passage, and they had promised to pay their aunt back the money, once they'd settled. A new and better life was promised. But not before Mrs Carey had given them a good Irish send-off. It would take her mind off the fact that she knew she would never set eyes on her daughter again, or cradle and comfort any grandchildren she might have.

She was a small, well-rounded, middle-aged woman, with greying hair and a very pleasant face. This woman had seen every aspect, both good and bad, that life could conjure up.

Over the years, she had given birth to seventeen children, of whom twelve were still living. She was a tough old boot and could be a force to be reckoned with if crossed. But kindness was her main virtue. Therefore, all the neighbours were invited to the going away party.

The Careys' lived in the cellar of Marys' tenement house. A

4Queenstown: now known as Cork city in Ireland

large cold room with four barred windows, at path level, that threw shadows around the room; this is where Mrs Carey had given birth to all of her children.

In the first throes of childbirth, on her last pregnancy, the women of the lane had gathered at the little cellar windows and peered down, worried as Annie wasn't a young one any longer. They called down to encourage her, that all would be well.

"Ye are doing grand, Annie", "Keep going, gal", "God bless you, Annie, "was shouted down through the cellar window in unity.

After one short hour, the screaming baby's wailing was heard throughout the tenements. Everyone cheered, hugged and blessed themselves. "Thanks be to god," they had all chorused.

Her birthing days behind her, she now had time for a party or two. So when the word spread that the Careys were to have a party: there was great excitement, anything to break up the monotony. On the day of the party, with the working day done, everyone rushed to wash their one and only blouse or shirt, which they then dried by the fire. Then they took turns in the tin bath, which had been dragged up from the lane. You had to be quick; other families were waiting for their turn to use the tin bath and hollered at the door for you to hurry up.

Mary had boiled the leaves of the rosemary plant and then let them cool, keeping the scented water to rinse her hair with it. She then tied it up with a red ribbon to match her newly dyed petticoat. She put on her clean white blouse and neckerchief and brushed her skirt. Mary and Catherine were excited as they set off down the stairs to the cellar room. Each secretly hoping the object of their desires would notice them.

The men had gathered by the water trough, everyone was in good form joking and laughing, excited at the chance to put their worries behind them, even if it was for just one night. John took special care to wash in the icy water and had even borrowed a cut throat blade to shave and shape his goatee; all the while secretly wondering if Mary would be there. He was sure she had smiled at him today. Taken by surprise, he hadn't responded. But he was sure now that she was as interested as he was.

As he entered the room, he immediately spotted Mary sitting in the corner with her brother who was chatting to a pretty, dark-haired girl with high cheekbones. Mary was listening intently to a story being told of failed risings and fallen heroes. When the storyteller finished, someone broke into song and everyone joined in the chorus, singing the wrong words, much to the annoyance of the singer, who cursed them, then decided to sing the song his way. John plucked up the courage and made his way over to talk to Mary. As he headed across the floor, he managed to trip over someone's outstretched leg and land partially in Mary's lap, startling the two girls. Pat reached out his hand and pulled John standing.

"John, is it?" Pat smiled.

"Aye," replied John going red with embarrassment. Pat introduced the two girls and then continued his conversation with Catherine. Mary sat tapping her feet to the music now being played, as John struggled for something to say. "Mary, is it?" John finally said.

"Tis," Mary said, trying not to look interested.

"So ye like dancing, do ya?" John asked, shouting over the music.

"Aye, I do; in fact, I'm a great dancer, ye know," Mary lied, trying to impress John.

Overhearing their conversation, Pat joined in, "Sure Mary's the best Irish dancer in the lane," he said, winking at John. "Sure why don't ya give us a twirl, Mary?" he teased.

"Ah no sure, I couldn't," said Mary, panicking. But before she could say another word, Pat, a little drunk, called for quiet.

"Hush! Now hush, my sister Mary is going to give us a wee twirl," he called as he pulled Mary to her feet and pushed her towards the middle of the floor. Mary glared at Catherine to help her, but Catherine just shrugged her shoulders and stared up at Pat. The fiddler picked up his fiddle and sat poised. Seeing no way out, Mary pointed her toe, as she had seen other dancers do, and the fiddler began to play a Slip Jig.

Mary jumped and kicked; she twirled and tapped her heels. Having no idea what the steps were, she just kept going, praying the crowd were too drunk to notice. John stood with his hand over his mouth, smiling. Pat was bent over Catherine, slapping his leg and laughing so hard he was spilling his drink. Mary prayed for the fiddler to finish, as she kicked her legs high showing all her newly dyed red petticoat.

Now Mary was a big-bosomed lady, and the more she jumped and kicked the more her breasts bounced and jiggled. This sent the crowd into a chorus of cheering and clapping, and this in turn made the fiddler play faster. John couldn't stand idly by and watch Mary, who was dying of embarrassment. He stepped into the middle of the floor and placed one arm around her waist. Raising one arm high, he began to dance with Mary.

Looking up at him gratefully, Mary followed his lead and they began to rotate in a circle.

John whispered, "When I nod, get ready to stop." John caught the fiddler's eye and then nodded to Mary to stop. With pointed toes and arms held high; they came to a standstill in the middle of the room.

The room went wild, calling, "More, Mary, more."

Mary panting heavily ran from the room, but not before she had slapped Pat hard on the back.

Mrs Carey was over like a shot to scold Pat. "Now, lad, ye knows full well single gals don't dance. Dat's no way to treat your sister. Gits some sense, me lad, or I'll box them ears off ya," she had threatened, while twisting one of his ears.

"Sorry, Mrs Carey, sure was just a bit of sport, it won't happen again, sure it won't. I meant no harm, Mrs, swear to god I didn't," gulped an embarrassed Pat.

"It had better not happen again, me lad, or I'll be having a word wit ya da. I'm watching ya,"she said, wagging her finger at him, as she made her way back to her seat. She lifted her Guinness to her lips, nodding for the fiddler to continue.

John left the noisy little room and made his way outside. There he found Mary leaning against the railings breathing heavily with her hands covering her face.

"There's the dancer now," John joked.

"Ah go on, so, have a good laugh, why don't ya?" Mary shouted at him angrily.

"I'm not laughing at all," said John, acting offended. "Sure I never seen dancing like it, swear to God I haven't," he said, putting his hand on his heart to show his sincerity. "I dunno, I thought we made a great team," he laughed.

Mary looked at him and tried not to laugh. John could see she was calming down. He proceeded to break a woodbine in half, lit both ends and handed one half to her, his finger briefly touching hers, sending electric sparks between them. She took it and sucked on it lightly, not looking at him.

"Well now, Mary Douglas, any chance ye would come walking with me sometime? If ya fancy it like?" asked John, kicking himself as that was not now he had planned to ask her.

"Well, ya cheeky rogue, one dance and ye think I'll go walking with ya, the cheek!" Mary scoffed, trying to sound offended and making to walk away from him.

"Jaysus, you're a hard woman so ye are, Mary Douglas. Cum now, don't be like that, I've liked ya for the longest time now. I just couldn't get to talk to ya at tall. Tis no one else, for me, Mary, God's truth." John affirmed this by crossing himself. "Go on, say ye will." John nudged her, thinking that he had messed everything up.

Mary couldn't believe her ears and turned back to look up into his dark eyes impure amazement. John looked down at her pretty face, her lips were parted slightly, and he smiled. "Tis only you, Mary," he said as he continued to stare into her eyes. Then without thinking, he quickly bent his head down and kissed her lightly on the lips.

A little startled, Mary laughed nervously, moving away. Then she cheekily replied, "Sure I thought ya'd never ask." As she made to leave, she looked back over her shoulder, "Tis only you, John," she called as she skipped back into the party.

Delighted, John stood there with the biggest smile on his face, shaking his head in wonder. "Tank ye, God," he said as he looked up into the night sky.

First thing the next day, Mary ran to find Catherine to tell her what had happened the night before. She hadn't been able to talk to her because of all the noise at the party and because Catherine had been hanging on to every slurred word Pat had uttered. So Mary had just sat with a little smile on her face all night. Pat was so drunk Mary had to carry him home. Now, she was bursting to tell her friend all about her first kiss.

"Well, you've done it now; ye do know dat, don't ya? You're feckin' pregnant now for sure," shouted a shocked Catherine at her, partly in fear and partly in jealousy. Pat hadn't even tried to hold her hand and here Mary was all kissed!

"Are ye sure? Don't ya have to be married to get a baby?" a petrified Mary asked.

"Sure! 'Course I'm sure, everyone knows dat's how it happens," explained Catherine, puffing herself up to make her point. "Now what ya going to do? For it's a sin, ya know, the priest will condemn ya at da Sunday Mass and sure everyone will ignore ya. You're fecked for sure," Catherine nodded solemnly.

Not having a mother of her own, Mary ran off crying to find Mrs Carey.

Mrs Carey, a little hung over from the night before, was none too pleased when a sobbing Mary had come calling about being kissed. She tried to calm Mary down as she sat holding her head in her hands.

"Jayus be quiet will ya, child? tis hurting me head, hush, child and I'll explain what happens. But only because you have no ma of your own!" she added. Mary sat listening as Mrs Carey explained the ins and outs of getting pregnant. The more Mrs Carey explained the sicker and bewildered Mary felt.

"Now that doesn't mean ye can go around kissing. Ah no! for tis the woman's job not to encourage the man. We women, ya see, have to be strong. Ya see men are da weak ones when it comes to the sex," counselled Mrs Carey, whispering the sex word.

Mary was mentally begging Mrs Carey to stop talking and ruining her precious moment with John.

"And me, girl, I'll have you know, tis a sin before God and his holy church to be doing the sex before marriage," preached Mrs Carey. "Now ya don't be encouraging that young John and we'll have no more of this kissing malarkey and there's an end to it, or you'll go to hell. Now mark me words," puffed Mrs Carey quite out of breath from scolding Mary. She blessed herself, satisfied that she'd done her duty as a catholic woman and had tried to save Mary's soul and keep her chaste.

"Now go on, feck off, will ye, me head's fit to burst." She sighed, taking out her clay pipe and lighting it to steady her nerves.

"Jayus the chislers of today, I'll never understand them, not if I live to be a hundred," she muttered to herself.

"Tanks, Mrs Carey," said a relieved Mary as she ran from the room to find Catherine.

"Jayus, that's flipping[5] awful, and in any ways, why would anyone do dat?. I'm never doing dat, *ugh!*" Catherine sat totally shocked as Mary explained what Mrs Carey had told her.

"Well, if in ya wants a baby, dat's what ye have to do," a traumatised Mary told Catherine gravely.

"No wonder there's so much moaning; it must hurt to high heaven. Tis a wonder anyone would wants a chiseller at tall if in ya have to do dat," said a disgusted Catherine.

Both girls sat and thought about it and, totally sickened and horrified, vowed that they wouldn't be doing the sex anytime soon.

"So if he kisses ya, will ye be slapping him away?" An eager Catherine asked.

"Oh Jayus, I surely will," lied Mary.

A delighted Catherine hugged her. "Dat's me girl."

Although Mary was delighted that kissing wouldn't get her pregnant, she wasn't so sure that if John kissed her again that she would be slapping him away. It had made her tummy do somersaults and that was too good to be wrong. As quickly as she

---

5Flipping: slang word for terrible or a soft curse word.

had been warned, she just as quickly put the act of getting pregnant out of her head and focused on the way she had felt when she had been kissed by John; even if it had just been briefly, it had been wonderful.

The following Sunday after mass, they did indeed go walking, with Catherine and Pat as chaperones much to Catherine's delight, as this meant she could spend time with Pat and get to know him. At the same time doing her duty and keeping Mary's good name intact. John brought a delighted Mary, a small posy of violets, which she later pressed into the back of her bible. He offered Mary his arm as they strolled down Sackville Street, his thumb rubbing her fingers ever so lightly, as they walked along. They stood and stared as if it was happening in slow motion, as finely dressed ladies and gentlemen, trotted by in their open-topped carriages. Their horses' heads held high. Their long manes like silk, brushed with such care, blowing in the breeze as they hurried by.

They made their way over Carlisle Bridge[6]. Just as, when they were still children, they threw stick boats over one side of the bridge and ran to see whose stick would go under the bridge first and out the other side. They gazed enviously into all the fine establishments on Grafton Street selling ladies' fine silk dresses and gentlemen's tweed suits. Sheepskin and leather gloves, lace handkerchiefs and beautiful bonnets trimmed with lace, with peacock feathers adorning the back of them. Items meant only for the wealthy, they could but dream. Then they made their way to Stephen's Green to sit and enjoy the sunshine. They were relaxed and happy in each other's company and talked and laughed as if they didn't have a care in the world. A brass band

---

[6]Carlisle Bridge: renamed O'Connell Bridge in 1882 in honour of Daniel O'Connell

was playing nearby on the newly erected bandstand. They sat nearby, so they could listen. Families and couples also stopped to enjoy the music. As the sun was setting, the warden's bell could be heard tolling. This was the signal that the park would be closing soon. The lamplighters with their long cane poles worked their way from lamp to lamp along the streets, spreading light into the darkness. Wearily, they made their way home tired but happy.

When the days got warmer, Mary and Catherine would pack a small picnic of bread and buttermilk and they would all head off to the Grand Canal. Once there they would pick a spot where the dragonflies hovered along the edge of the river banks, and sunshine danced on the surface of the water. There they would spread their coats and lay down to be warmed by the sun which embraced them, like a thousand warm fingers. John and Pat had taken off their shirts. This sent the girls into shy giggles. While balancing on a fallen tree, the boys dived into the canal, calling for the girls to join them.

"Go way will ye, we're not going in dere, feck off," the girls had giggled.

Taking revenge, they raced out and shook themselves over the two girls, who screeched and went running, the lads chasing after them. Later, they kicked a ball about, which had been made from old rags tightly wound round and round and covered in a tar substance till it was rock hard and fit to be kicked. The lads, weaving and dodging the girls, ran circles around them as they tried to get a kick of the ball. Hampered by their long skirts, they were often sent flying and soon gave up, leaving the two men to play by themselves. Summer days seemed long and hot. On days like these, hard times and hard work were put to the back of their minds.

As time passed, the four of them became close and looked forward to their Sundays together. But every summer must turn to Autumn.

As winter set in, they would meet in Mrs Carey's to play cards and other times they sat on the steps of the tenement house and just chatted under the moonlight. At Halloween, they chiselled creepy faces on large turnips and made Jack-o'-lanterns for the children of the street to put in their windows or doorways to frighten Stingy Jack[7] and other wandering spirits from entering their homes. John was a great storyteller and would sit and weave stories out of thin air. Some had ghosts and goblins, others had banshees[8] and leprechauns; whichever it was the children of the street would not sleep that night, much to the annoyance of their mothers and John would get an earful from the women of the lane the next day for scaring the bejesus out the chiselers'.

In early December, they had a rare day out at the Smock Alley Theatre. They went to the matinee and crowded into the penny stalls to watch a comedy show, which mocked the upper-class gentry and their way of life. There were deep undertones of the growing dissatisfaction with the British government. The actors wore oversized costumes and outrageous makeup, exaggerating every gesture with great gusto. Mary and Catherine thought they would wet their knickers, they laughed so much. Loud boos were called out whenever the villain appeared and old cabbages and rotten fruit were thrown on stage, which they had collected as they passed the fruit and vegetable market of Smithfield. The two men were delighted that they had made the right choice to bring them here. They would be in the good books

---

[7]Stingy Jack: A spirit, who roams the earth looking for his soul that the devil had taken

[8]Banshee: In Irish Legend, a female spirit whose wailing warns of a death in the house

for weeks. But for John that wouldn't last long. John had been working longer hours coming up to Christmas. Mary had seen less and less of him. He exhausted; he had just collapsed into bed at the end of each day. She became worried that he was tired of her, so she set her mind to confront him. The following Sunday, John was very quiet, he could barely keep his attention on the conversation, he was so tired. Losing her temper, Mary shouted at him, "Jayus, John, if ye don't want to be here, then feck off home, would ya?"

Startled, John suddenly perked up. "Of Course, I want to be here. Sorry, Mary, I've been working extra hours, it's busy around Christmas, dat's all."

Mary wasn't having that excuse. "Are you sure now, John Le Petit?" She questioned him hand on hip. "Are ye sure ya haven't got some flussie on the side that's keeping ya busy and making ya tired? Well, go on then, spit it out and don't be wasting my time."

John wanted to laugh, but he kept a straight face. She was pretty when she was angry, eyes all flashing, her head all haughty. He reached for her hand nervously. "Mary, don't ye know tis only you? There will only ever be you."

John took a deep breath, heart pounding and still holding her hand, he kissed her fingers .He spoke slowly and quietly, "Mary, I'm a simple man and I don't have much to offer ya, but I'll always work hard and I'll stand by your side no matter what. We can face each thing God throws at us, together, and ifin, ye can't face things, and then I'm strong enough for both of us. What I'm trying to say is: Would ye be me wife? Ifin you'll have me, dat is?" John asked with his head down, rubbing her hands, fearing she'd say no.

Mary threw her arms around his neck and hugged him close.

"Tanks be to God, I thought ya didn't want me no more, and yes John Le Petit, I'd love to marry ya," she said. As she pulled back a little, she put her two hands on either side of his face. He was smiling. She pulled his face down to her sand kissed him right there on the steps of the tenements.

Eddie had been approving of the match. He liked John and more importantly he had never seen Mary so happy. But he had made John work at asking for her hand. He secretly smiled, as a nervous John explained his intentions and had gone redder and redder as he finally got around to asking Eddie for her hand.

"And Mary feels the same, I take it?" Eddie had asked, already knowing the answer.

John couldn't confirm it strongly enough. "She surely does, sir. We luv each other, there no doubt, we surely do, Mr Douglas."

"Well, luv won't feed and clothe her?" Eddie questioned, puffing on his pipe.

"I will work hard every day. She'll never go hunger or be homeless, as God is my witness. I swear to ye dat tis true. I'll never do her any harm, sir," he had strongly responded.

Eddie had stood in silence for a long, exaggerated time. John had sat, nearly forgetting to breathe. Twisting his cap in his hands, Eddie decided to put the boy out of his misery and stood up and took John's hand. "Welcome to the family, son, and ya can call me Eddie."

John was so relieved; he kept hold of Eddie's hand and shook it. Letting out a deep breath, John said, "Tank ya, sir, tank ya, don't worry about a thing. I'll take good care of her. I'll work hard, don't fret, it will be grand, sir, for sure."

John had babbled on and on until finally Eddie had pulled his hand away. "I know, son, tis fine, now go on now, I'm sure she's waiting for me answer."

John put his hat back on and nodded again at Eddie and ran to tell Mary who was waiting anxiously in the lane. Mary had been overjoyed and John had lifted her up and swung her around and around. Neither could wait for their life together to begin.

John worked hard that following year, saving every penny that he could. He took extra work in the brewery at night, working with the dray horses. Mucking out the stables brushing down the horses and filling up their hay and water for the night. One evening, as he was mucking out, he heard the clunk of metal. Pushing the hay away, there before him was a horse shoe. He gathered it up and smiled; he would nail it to the door of his and Papas' room, for Mary would join them there once they were married, and this would bring them luck. He kissed it and put it in his pocket, humming quietly, he carried on mucking out the stables, content that this was a sign they would indeed be happy.

John had gone to Fitzwilliam's Street earlier that year where there was a pawnshop. If items weren't collected in time, they were resold. You could buy them at a discounted price. He had selected a thin bronze band with a delicate Celtic design going around it, costing three shillings and sixpence and had been paying off the price of the ring, whenever he had an extra shilling. Most women didn't have wedding bands, but John wanted the world to know that Mary was his and planned to surprise her on their wedding day. When the priest whispered 'Is there a ring?' not expecting there to be one, John would proudly produce the small bronze ring. He knew Mary would be overjoyed.

Mary too had had a busy year, along with looking after her father and two brothers she had taken in piece work, sewing and doing fine embroidery, and mending. Items of clothing belonging to one of the big houses that circled Stephen's Green. Long into the night, she would sit stitching by the light of a tallow candle, but with every stitch she sewed, she knew it brought her closer to her desire, which was to have a white cotton hood trimmed with lace. Once she was married, she would wear her hair pinned up under the hood. She longed for a white cotton neckerchief to make her feel more mature like the other married women; and she would embroider tiny violets at the corners of it. Even more important: a nice cotton nightshift for her wedding night. She stitched all night to buy new sheets (well, maybe not new but as good as) for her new home, and every stitch would be worth it. Mrs Carey had given her a beautiful cotton tablecloth which she had embroidered with apples and ivy going along the edges. Mary had gone to the clothes stall at the market and after haggling with the stall owner for ten minutes, she had managed to buy John a coarse linen shirt for their wedding day and herself a blouse with three tiny buttons at the throat and a lace trim for sixpence. They were in great condition and Mary had run home thrilled with herself.

The banns of marriage were read out at church each Sunday, three months before the wedding. John and Mary had to meet with the priest once a month to talk about the sanctity of marriage, the place of a dutiful wife and the duty of the God-fearing husband. But, above all, the church expected them to go forth and procreate to keep the word of God alive in the next generation and bring each child up a catholic. After each meeting, with the fear of God in them, they would walk home in silence not even daring to kiss each other goodnight.

All in all, it had been a hard year, each working towards the same goal. That they cared deeply for each other was obvious to everyone. As they were still considered minors, Eddie and Papa would be their sponsors and Patrick and Catherine their witnesses. By summer even Patrick had caught the marriage fever and had proposed to Catherine. They planned to get married the following year. So the four friends would have everything in common and this would keep them close to each other whether it was good or bad times.

Wedding Day, 4 November 1866

On the evening, before the wedding, the Bride's job was to cook a goose for their meal the next day. Traditionally, it meant: once the goose was cooked for the groom, there was no going back. The deal was done. So Mary had cooked the goose that her father had supplied for them. He had managed to get it at a good price with a bit of haggling and it would be their wedding feast. Mary and Catherine dressed the room with ivy. Then they dragged the tin bath from the yard. Everyone was made to leave, so Mary could have a relaxing bath. But her head raced with the events of the next day and she was both excited and scared. Catherine washed Mary's hair in lavender water and tied it with strips of material to curl her hair; after tomorrow, it would be pinned up in a bun, as was the case with every married woman. But for tomorrow, she would wear it loose under her white cotton cap. Catherine surprised Mary with a posy of ivy and holly that she had wound together with a white ribbon tied in a bow. It sat ready for the next day in a cup of water. Mary would carry it with her down the aisle along with the horseshoe John had found in the stables. He had polished it up and given it to her to carry on her special day. Down the lane, John was doing much the same thing except Patrick and a few lads were drinking and teasing him, so were of little help.

"Well, that's it for you, lad, you're surely fecked now. Your freedom gone with the wind, your goose is cooked, you'll be limping around once the auld ball and chain is placed on your leg. Sure God help ya." They had nudged each other, teasing John.

John just smiled. "I'm more than happy, tis all I've ever wanted and sure I got the best in the lane, so what's to complain about?"

"Good answer, John," nodded Pat.

The teasing was all meant in good humour and was supposed to keep the groom calm and soothe any last-minute nerves. But John was so sure of what he wanted. He was relaxed and happy, so he laughed with them and enjoyed the banter[9].

Sunday, 4 November, dawned bright and crisp. Mary had been up early to get ready and busied herself tidying up to steady her nerves. Her father hugged her close and then stood back to admire her. "You're as pretty as a picture. I just wish ya ma could see ya.. Ya looks so pretty. I'm happy for you, Mary, I like John and I think he'll be a good husband to ye, so I'll toast your happiness and wish ya well," he said, raising his glass and taking a sup of ale.

"Tanks, Da, I luvs ya," Mary replied, trying to hold back the tears, for after today she would live with John and not her dad.

Eddie hugged her. "I luvs ya too, pet," he said hoarsely and handed her a sixpence to put in her shoe for luck. Mary tucked it into her shoe and kissed him lightly on the forehead. John arrived soon afterwards and Mary thought she'd melt, he looked so handsome.

Ireland being a very superstitious country, nothing was left to chance, so the couple sat to eat an oatmeal and salt porridge. Neighbours called in on their way to the mass. There were

---

[9]Banter: friendly, playful teasing

handshakes and warm wishes. Mrs Carey came in and hugged and kissed them both, her eyes filled with tears. "You are a lovely couple and I wish use every happiness." Then she went on to preach to them about marriage. "Now marriage isn't easy, ya has to work at it," she counselled. "But you will always have each other from this day on, May God bless ya with lots of babies." She toasted them, raising her glass.

She gave Mary a lace hanky which would be made into a bonnet for her first born when the time came. Mary hugged her fondly, hiding the tears. They all headed to the church of St Michin as the bells rang out for mass. After mass was said, the priest called on any couples who were to be married to come to the altar. There were only two couples that Sunday. They stood solemnly as he told them of their duties and the responsibility as a married couple. They smiled shyly, holding hands and looked into each other's eyes as they said their vows to each other. The priest never asked for a ring, so John had to prompt him.

"You have a ring?" He mocked as he stared down his nose as if he had smelled a foul stench.

But not deterred, John produced the bronze ring. The priest placed the ring on the bible with a sneer and blessed it. John took it and placed it on Mary's finger who had stood there open-mouthed and silently crying with joy. Pronouncing them married, the crowd cheered and John leaned forward and kissed Mary. She shyly responded and took his hand as they made their way down the aisle, their friends and family joined them and they headed back to Eddie's room to feast and enjoy their first day as a married couple. The small party ate and drank happily. This time Mary danced as a married woman and not a tut was whispered from anyone. Some of the neighbours came by and soon they were all singing and making merry. The party sang and danced and toasted the newlyweds long into the night. At some point later in the evening, John had taken Mary's hand and they slipped away to their own room in Mary's Lane. Papa had made other arrangements that night, to give the newlyweds some privacy.

Mary stood in the middle of the room remembering Mrs Carey's words on what went on in the bedroom. She was both scared and excited all in one feeling. John watched her for a while then took her hand and sat her down. Kneeling down, he removed her shoes, the forgotten sixpences rolling across the floor, they both giggled. Then he removed her bonnet.

"Welcome home, Mrs Le Petit." He smiled up at her.

She kept her head down, staring at the wedding ring.

"Are ya pleased with da ring, Mary?" John asked.

"Tis perfect, John, tank ya. tis so special," she breathed.

"Tis you that's special, Mary," John had replied tenderly as he kissed her fondly on the forehead.

John had got an extra pallet and new flour sacks and had filled them with fresh straw. Remembering her new sheets, Mary jumped up and started spreading the sheets on the straw mattress while John made them some tea. She unpacked her meagre belongings and placed her China teapot on the mantelpiece. He then broke a woodbine in half and lit both ends. Mary happily sat by the fire drinking her tea, as John tenderly rubbed her feet. They smoked their cigarettes recounting what a grand day it had been. Later, both happy and relaxed, John had carried her to their bed. He kissed her tenderly and whispered in her ear, "Tis only you, Mary."

Mary smiled in the dark and gave her usual response "Tis only you, John." Only this time, it was said with the knowledge that he was hers and hers alone. For John, the dream he had of holding and loving her had finally come true.

The next morning, they awoke entwined in each other's arms. Waking with a little start, Mary at first didn't realise where she was and then she remembered John was her husband. So she lay there contentedly as he stroked her hair. John lying with Mary in his arms was the happiest man alive. He held her close and then they made love again and again, as only young lovers can. When hunger got the better of them, Mary proceeded to make them their first breakfast, while John nailed the horseshoe to the door to ensure them good luck. They began their new life like everyone else, constantly looking for work and constantly struggling. But most of all, they were happy and still getting to know each other. Things were easier in the beginning as they only had themselves and Papa to worry about. Every day, John and Papa went looking for work, while Mary cooked and washed and cleaned for them and then headed over to her father's to do the same.

Sometimes, Catherine called over, all questions about being married, and then her turn to walk down the aisle came. She told Mary that she was glad it wasn't as bad as Mrs Carey had described, in fact it was rather pleasant. They both laughed at that, neither giving any secrets away. Each night, John and Mary lay in each other's arms and talked and giggled quietly so as not to wake Papa, who lay at the other side of the partitioned curtain. The harsh and cold world was left at the front door till morning. The night was for them and them alone, this is where they were happiest together alone.

1856. Marriage solemnized at the Roman Catholic Chapel of St Brendan, St Ours City in the Registrar's District of Schull C/4 in the Union of North Dublin, In the County of City of Dublin.

No.	When Married	Name and Surname	Age	Condition	Rank or Profession	Residence at the Time of Marriage	Father's Name and Surname	Rank or Profession of Father
198	Nov 4th 1856	John Joseph O'Ralaghan	Thirty	Bachelor	Civil Patentee	48 Henry Street	John O'Ralaghan	Etown
		Mary Doyle	Minor	Spinster	None	6 Swift's Row	Edwd Doyle	Painter

Married in the Roman Catholic Chapel of St Brendan, St Ours CC according to the Rites and Ceremonies of the Roman Catholic Church by me,
C. Morris C.C.

This Marriage was solemnized between us { John Joseph O'Ralaghan / Mary Doyle her X mark } in the Presence of us { L. Stirling &c / Mary Roche Doyle }

1856. Marriage solemnized at the Roman Catholic Chapel of St Brendan, St Ours, In the Registrar's District ...

John and Mary's Wedding Certificate

Les Enfant

He wasn't really a big drinker, but when William was born, boy how he had celebrated! Mary was safe in the Lying in Hospital[10] in Britain Street[11] and so puffed up with pride that he had produced a male heir. A son, to carry on the Le Petit name. He headed to the nearest pub on the corner of Capel Street and toasted his new son's head to a drunken chorus of, "Good on ya.! God bless da littlein" from the crowded little pub. The drink flowed, and soon Ireland's woes, were played out in song. Eventually, they had grown tired of his revelry and had thrown him out. Staggering he made his way home. Muttering and chatting to himself, he had collapsed fully clothed onto the straw mattress. His father had heard him come in and peaked behind the sheet curtain that partitioned the room. "Well, garson (boy) what we get?" his father had asked eagerly.

"A son! Papa, a son!" he said, raising his arms to heaven.

"Tres bien" (very good). His father nodded in approval. "Maintenant dors mon fils."(Now sleep, my son)But John had already passed out.

In the cold light of day, John had to face the fact that he had drunk all of their money and there was no rent money left. Ashamed of himself he had puked and puked in the lane, to the disgust of all the women out doing their washing.

"Aw Jayus, John, for Christ sake," they shouted.

---

[10]Lying in hospital: now known as The Rotunda Hospital
[11]Britain Street: now known as Parnell Street

"My apologies, ladies," he had shamefully muttered as he tripped over the pigs that roamed the lane. How would he face Mary? The shame! (For it was every man's duty to look after his family)He was not like some men who beat their wife or drank all the wages. He had prided himself on that, yet here he was, as bad as them.

"How could ya?" Mary had cried as he picked her up from the hospital, little William tucked up in her shawl. "Jayus! John!" She had screamed. "What do we do now?"

He had bent his head in shame, his temples throbbing. He stood for a moment then he broke a woodbine in half, lit both ends and handed one to Mary, not looking at her. Mary stood with the baby safely in her shawl and fumed.

"Any chance of a quick peek at the wee fella?" ventured John.

Mary shot John an annoyed look. Then reluctantly, she lifted the shawl away from the baby's face. John stared at the little wonder lying in Mary's arms with his little lace bonnet that Mary had made from her wedding handkerchief.

"Jayus, Mary, he's mighty[12]! Aw he's a corker[13] so he is," he gushed. "Just grand. Howa ya young William?" he cooed, as little fingers instinctively curled around his. Mary nearly purred like a kitten. She was so happy, forgetting she was angry with John. The two of them just stood there staring down at their precious baby boy. John lifted Mary's fingers to his lips. "Tis only you, Mary," he said as he kissed them. "I'm truly sorry, Mary."

"Tis only you, John," she replied, everything forgotten.

They struggled that week, but with the help of Papa they managed. John walked the streets of Dublin searching and

---

[12]Mighty: extraordinary
[13]Corker: (dated slang) meaning remarkable

begging till he got a day's work, he'd even found some coal lying on the street that had tumbled from a coal cart as it had taken a corner. He scrambled to collect as much as possible. Slowly, Mary forgave him.

What a bonny lad William was! Good and healthy. No one could deny that William was the apple of his father's eye. As for William, he followed his dad around like a little puppy always at his side, and a special bond grew between them. Just before their second child arrived, John's father had become very ill; his breathing had become much laboured and he coughed up phlegm continuously. John feared for his father's health and that of Mary's. Having no money for a doctor, Mary had boiled onions for her father-in-law, which was good for the chest. She had held his head over the steaming pot for him to inhale and then fed him the soupy onions. But nothing helped and it was with reluctance that they decided to take him to the workhouse where at least, he would get some medical attention. His father was too weak to walk unaided. So, wrapping one arm around his father's back and then under his arm, John had carried him. Mary wrapped a scarf around Papa's neck; she had kissed and hugged him. They all cried, for they knew that he would never leave that dreaded place.

"I'll pray for ya, Papa John," Mary wept.

William had clung to his leg. "No, Papa John! No go!" he had whaled and cried with no real idea of what was happening except that his beloved Papa was going somewhere without him. At the gates of the workhouse, John cupped his father's face and kissed him on the forehead.

"Je t'aime pere`re," (I love you, Father) he whispered. "I'll see ya soon," John lied.

His father smiled, John never spoke his ancestral tongue and he knew it was his way of showing his father he had not forgotten his roots. Coughing and spluttering, he managed to say, "Don't – tout bon. (All good)I'll be back."

At the gates to the workhouse, John handed his father over to the men at the entrance of the workhouse. He stood, chest-heaving, watching while they carried him in. His papa out of sight, he had cried uncontrollably, great sobs escaping his throat, tears streaming down his face. He knew he would never see him again. For twelve days later, he died of pneumonia.

After William, Mary hadn't seemed to be able to hold a baby in her belly, but in September 1869 she again gave birth. In honour of his father who had recently passed away, their second son was called John. With Papa John gone, they just couldn't afford the bigger room, so they had reluctantly moved to a smaller room in Greek Street.

Little John at eleven months old was crawling and making words. When John would return in the evenings, baby John with his grubby face and innocent eyes would stretch up his arms to be picked up, gurgling and smiling. John would kiss his neck and shoulders, in quick succession. The baby twisted every which way to get away from his cold lips.

"He loves that, Da." William would laugh.

"Does he know, and how about ye, do ye luv it?" John would say pouncing on William and kissing him all over. William would squeal with laughter.

"What about yer ma, does she luv it?" John would grab Mary and kiss and nuzzle her neck while she wiggled and laughed trying to get away.

"Go away will ye, ya eejit," she'd say, struggling to straighten her apron over her swollen belly.

In August 1870, little John suddenly passed away from a raging fever that racked his little body for days. Beads of sweat clung to his brow. His hair was soaked, and he had just moaned in distress. Eventually, it was just too much for his little body to take and one morning he just wasn't with them anymore. Their grief was intense. With Mary already pregnant, John feared for her wellbeing and sat rocking and cradling her as she wailed and cried long into the night; nothing could calm her. William also felt the loss of his little brother; he had been a loving and protective brother towards him and would feel John's loss like a pang in his chest for a very long time.

"Sure you're young, you'll have more, there's plenty of time" is what people had said, as if there was no loss to feel. Babies came and babies died, such was the way of their world.

By December 1870, Anne was born only to die two months later. Fearing the worst, Mary had run to the church and asked the priest to quickly baptise Anne. For days, Mary had sat rocking her back and forth as she dampened cold beads of perspiration from her brow. Hour after endless hour not knowing what else to do, she had tried to spoon water into her mouth. But Anne was just too weak; she couldn't feed and quietly moaned, her little body jerking periodically, until she had lost consciousness and had silently sunk into the peaceful sleep of death as only the innocent can do. Again they went begging to the Sisters of Charity for the price of a burial, which they would never refuse, as every child was a child of God, especially a baptised one!

"Where is God? Have we not tried to live a good Christian life? Why do ye punish us, lord?" A grief-stricken John had ranted to an unknown entity.

A year later, in early May, when the consumption[14] or (the galloping consumption as it was known) swept through the tenements, they decided to move again; this time back to Mary's Lane. By now, Mary had given birth to a second daughter named Mary .But things were no better; their room was cold and damp, the lack of food and the constant search for work was debilitating.

---

[14] Consumption or tuberculosis: Disease caused by bacteria that attacks the lungs.

By the time baby Mary was two, things were at breaking point. Mary and John had to make the decision to let Mary's brother Pat and his wife Catherine take little Mary to live with them. Mary was close to her brother and Catherine was like the sister she had never had, so visiting little Mary would be easy. Pat and Catherine doted on the child. She was like a ray of sunshine, if not a little mischievous. They were happy to care for her. Not having any living children of their own at the time. They had suggested it many times as a short-term solution. Eventually, John and Mary, having no other choice, had agreed.

This would leave John free to look for work. Mary could rest and get stronger. They hoped it was temporary and that they would soon be in the position to bring her home. "Tis just temporary", "Tis the right thing to do", they had reassured each other. The alternative was the child dying from malnutrition.

Mentally battered and bruised, the couple continued to struggle, but made the decision that for now there would be no more children.

Young William had not had any schooling, because they had needed him to work when there was work. Which when he did attend school resulted in him getting his ears boxed by the headmaster for having little reading skills or even less arithmetic. So, John tried his best to teach him what he knew to make up for the time spent away from school. He knew it was important to know how to read and write so he made the effort whenever he could. John would spend some evenings teaching William to write his name and that of his mother and father. He even helped him learn his ABCs. Mary couldn't read nor write, but she embroidered letters on a piece of sack cloth, copying what John had written, so William could practice when John wasn't around. She even learned some of the letters herself, but quickly forgot again, having no use for writing. But she did learn to write her own name, something she was very pleased at having accomplished.

They continued to visit Mary often and she stayed with her parents on special occasions. Constantly hoping to bring Mary back home one day, when they could afford a better room.

What a little princess she was with a button nose and an infectious laugh. Graced with the sweetest nature, she had captured everyone's heart. The family made an extra effort to celebrate special occasions by always being together.

On a cold April day, Pat arrived at their little room, his eyes red and swollen. He had sobbed uncontrollably when he gave them the news that at four and half years old, little Mary had passed away from convulsions[15]. They felt their world dissolve from under their feet. Pat and Catherine were inconsolable; Mary had been loved by them, as if she was their own child. Their sense of bewilderment was beyond anything they had experienced before. Tormented, they asked, "Why had God forsaken them? What had they done to deserve this? How could life ever be the same?" These questions remained unanswered.

With the work situation getting no better, they moved again to a cheaper room in Bull Lane. It was close to the cellar, very dark and damp with little ventilation. Bugs crept along the walls and rats nibbled at their toes. Every pane of glass in the windows were either broken or cracked .But for now, they had a roof over their heads.

In desperation, John sought out a dentist who would buy a healthy tooth from him. This could be fatal if any infection set in afterwards, but John felt he was young and healthy and times were really hard. The dentist or for the most part (the local barber) gave John a small amount of laudanum[16] and then

---

[15]Convulsions: a condition which causes the muscles to contract uncontrollably, caused by specific chemicals in the blood

[16]Laudanum: An alcoholic solution containing morphine and prepared from opium used as a painkiller

proceeded with a dental key to remove his front incisor, which he would sell on to some wealthy client (they liked real teeth in their dentures). In return for the tooth, John received a guinea, a swollen mouth and a lot of pain. Mary was horrified when she saw John's face.

"John Le Petit, are ye mad? Never! do such a foolish thing again. What in God's name would we do if anything happened to you?" She had scolded him.

To stop any infection, she made him wash his mouth out with salt in warm water "We will get by and besides, I luv dis face, the way it tis, teeth and all." She had pushed his head away and shook her head in disbelief at what he'd done just to put food on the table.

After that, John took whatever work he could find no matter how little it paid. Sometime later, quite by accident, Mary found herself again pregnant.

They were pleased, but also worried as to how they would manage. Mary was weak and sick through most of the pregnancy. Mrs Carey had kept her supplied with thin soup and milky tea and had helped Mary throughout, as much as she could, and John was extremely grateful for that. They breathed a sigh of relief when Mary gave birth to Julia in July 1879. They were both delighted and happy that mother and baby had made it. However, Julia was a weak and sickly child and not expected to live. She was baptised quickly, but sadly passed away in September 1879.

"So much for the Catholic Church teaching ya that a child thrives once it's baptised," a disillusioned John had scornfully remarked. There and then vowing never to set foot in a church again, and he never did.

Reeling from Julia's death, they consoled each other as best they could. Trying to drag themselves out of bed each day was a physical and mental struggle. But having no other choice they carried on. They still had to pay rent and to eat and then there was

William who needed them now more than ever. Mary fell into a deep despondency. With the loss of each child, the ability to love unconditionally dwindled, replaced by a deep-set fear of unbearable pain and the girl with the fire in her eyes and the strut in her step slowly started to disappear, never to return. She suffered with bouts of depression that would plague her for the rest of her life.

Soon afterwards, John started getting work as a labourer, thanks to his friend Patrick Fitzgerald. They decided to move back to Mary's Lane, where it was less damp and there were no bugs or biting rats. Mary would be closer to neighbours he had known all of her life. John felt this would be of some help and support to her, and hoped that their misfortunes and traumas were in the past. He begged an unhearing God to somehow bring Mary back to him and William so they could start over. For the thing he feared most was that she would never be herself again. But even when he was begging God to help them, his heart wasn't in that prayer; he just couldn't believe in a god that could cause so much pain and suffering. He knew that they were not alone in the grief of losing their children. All around them, families buried their own. It was a daily occurrence in the tenements. But when it happens to you, the only thing you can think of is your own loss and John was getting beaten down with all the tragedies they kept suffering.

Saturday, 11 October 1879

It was so cold and damp in their room in Mary's Lane, no fire was lighting. Yet Mary sat in her night shift, wrapped in a fringed shawl right by it. John heaved himself up from the straw mattress, ran his hands through his untidy hair and struggled to put on his trousers. Still Mary didn't move, she looked haggard in the morning light that streamed through the dirty window. John bent to take out the ashes, remembering that they must be kept because they could be sold on when the rag and bone man came calling ;it seemed everything had a value, except human life. He used a small bit of kindling to get the fire going and slowly added turf. He looked about for water; there was none. So, taking the water bucket in one hand and the piss pot in the other; he made his way to the yard. There he filled the wooden bucket with water and emptied the piss into the waste barrel, which would be taken down river to be used for fertiliser when the night soil men came. While there, he washed his face and hands roughly in the water trough, it was icy cold and a shiver ran through him. Then he climbed back up the stairs and opened the door quietly, so as not to wake William. Filling the old iron kettle, which hung from a bar over the crude brick fireplace, he placed it over the now burning turf fire. He cut two slices of stale bread and toasted them over the flames. When they turned brown, he buttered them with some lard. Reaching for two chipped cups from the shelf, he proceeded to make some tea and still Mary had not moved, just sat there like she was stuck in a trance. When the tea had brewed, he added a small drop of milk, as there wasn't much to be had and he wanted to leave some for William when he awoke. He handed the cup of tea and a slice of bread to Mary, who slowly moved as if just noticing John. She tried to give a small smile but nothing showed on her face, just her eyebrows moved a little. John gently touched her shoulder in comfort, then sat and ate his bread and sipped his tea in silence. He nudged Mary with his foot and gestured towards the tea and bread.. "Eats up, luv." She nodded and made a feeble attempt to nibble the bread.

John stared into the fire lost in thought. Then he tipped the remainder of his tea down his throat and stood up. He reached for his coat from the bed, which served as a blanket at night.

"Aw feck it, ya little devil." He sighed.

William had put his two legs inside the arms of the coat, so it couldn't be pulled off him during the night by his freezing parents. John wouldn't have minded but it was the good army coat he'd found in the park while he'd been searching for conkers with William under the oak tree.

There it was, a British army wool corded coat, just there for the taking! *'Now ifin you need a coat, you wouldn't be leaving it behind for someone to take, so it mustn't be wanted,'* John had debated with himself. As quick as lightning, he had whipped it up and put it under his own ragged coat and taken it home. What a bit of luck! Surely god had wanted him to have it.

Mary had skilfully removed the buttons labels and cuffs and lapels to disguise the fact that it was an army coat and it was the warmest item of clothing John had ever owned. Not only had he a new coat, but Mary had also sold the buttons to the traveling dealer for two shillings and they had a feast that night of a small bit of ham with cabbage and potatoes washed down with buttermilk. They thought they'd died and gone to heaven, John recalled the scene in their little tenement room. There were smiles of contentment and full bellies.

"We're like kings, Da!" William had shouted, rubbing his belly; Mary and John had smiled contentedly, and even baby John had gurgled happily beside a homely turf fire.

Now William was snuggled up in the old army coat, his own worn-out coat lying unused for there was little heat left in it. Only holes remained where there had once been tweed. He hated to take it, because William would be cold and might wake. So he pulled on his old coat and consoled himself: *Sure I'll be warm enough once I git's working.* He looked down at William and stroked his hair lightly. He was a good lad; despite his youth, he tried hard to bring in an extra shilling. He most certainly would be their last. Even though they were still young, Mary surely couldn't bear to lose another child. He turned around to look at her.

"Mary," he started to say. She looked up at him, slowly with eyes so full of tears ready to fall, pleading with him to make it better. John just stood and stared; he could find no words of comfort that would mend a broken heart. It had been a month now since little Julia had passed away: forever in the arms of our lord and life would never be the same. A sickly child from the time she was born, they had hurried to get her baptised, but to no avail. Poor little Julia had lasted only two months upon this earth. The child had taken one last ragged breath, and she was still. With all her babies gone and only William left, Mary just hadn't the strength to pull herself back from the edge. Helpless and weary, John was at a loss to how to help her.

John stood over Mary looking down at his cap, twisting it with his fingers over and over. But he could find no words of reassurance and Mary turned her face away. He made to leave that little room, now warmed by the glowing fire, for he had work in Glasnevin Cemetery and if it worked out he could be there for several weeks, that was unheard of, nobody ever got a few weeks work! All thanks to his friend Patrick Fitzgerald who had put in a good word for him, he had landed this bit of work and it should be enough to sustain them, at least for a little while.

John broke a woodbine in half, lit both halves and handed one to Mary. Taking it, Mary nodded to him in thanks. Then with one last look back, he said, "Don't let the lad leave without some breakfast, he's to look for wood. Tell him to try the market; he might even get some work while he's there." Mary never answered.

John hesitated for a second, holding the door open. Turning, he softly whispered, "Tis' only you, Mary."

After a moment, Mary responded, "Only you, John." Satisfied, John closed the door behind him.

Stepping out into the bright sunshine, it was surprisingly pleasant for October; still, John let out a shiver and wrapped the collar of his coat around his neck. Going to Glasnevin brought back some of the saddest memories John had ever had. Remembering each baby; John, Ann, Mary and then little Julia, Feeling the weight of each tiny pine coffin on his shoulder. Mary, overcome with grief, hadn't accompanied him. He had carried them through the streets of Dublin not wanting anyone else to touch them, he had needed to hold on to them for as long as possible, not wanting to say goodbye. He crossed paths with women who blessed themselves and prayed. Happened on men, who doffed their hat's. They had probably made the same journey themselves at some time. John had kept his cap well down over his forehead and carried on, all the way to the gates of Glasnevin Cemetery.

After a small ceremony of prayers, he had handed each baby over to be buried in a pauper's grave[17], along with thousands of Dublin's poor. This was the most degrading thing of all, not to be able to afford to bury your kin[18] with respect and dignity.

The parish had to pay for the actual burial, but no marker was there to say that they had ever existed. The shame was crushing.

Such memories were hard to remember, so they were pushed to the back of the mind. With life a constant circle of looking for work, paying your rent and trying to get food, there was no time to dwell on the horrors that had befallen them.

John trudged along the already busy streets of a sleepy Dublin, waking to face another day of wheeling and dealing. The cries of street hawkers[19] filled the still air as they walked the streets with barrows filled with anything from cockles and mussels to flowers and fruit or vegetables, Baskets with ribbon or a little lace and various curiosities. Horses and carts trotted up and down the cobbled streets ready to sell their wares. The hot breaths of the horses mixed with the slight fog rising up from the stinking river Liffey. It would take him forty minutes to reach Glasnevin and he quickened his step down along the canal and across the docks. The roar of voices shattered his thoughts as men hurriedly loaded or unloaded the big ships tied up at the docks.

All sorts of goods were traded here. The stench of livestock caught in his throat and made him wretch. He covered his nose and mouth and hurried on. He joined up with Patrick Fitzgerald who had spotted him and stopped to wait for him to catch up.

---

[17]Pauper's grave: grave paid for by either church or government, because the deceased is too poor to afford to pay
[18]Kin: family
[19]Hawkers: vendor of merchandise that can be easily transported

"All right, Murray?" asked Pat with smoky breath from the cold.

"Grand, Pat, what's on for today?" John asked, falling into step with him.

"This foreman is a tight git, he'll have ya sweating buckets in no time. The church has to be moved yesterday, if ya gits me meaning," Pat winked continuing, "The pillars are to come down today or he'll have a Mickey fit[20]. So the contractors want us to get a move on. They want to have the grave plots available as soon as possible for the bloody Prodys[21]. So as when they come visiting the graves, they then can go for a nice pleasant stroll around the Botanic Gardens, he mocked in a posh voice. "Did ya ever hear the feckin like of it? It would only happen in Ireland, move a Catholic Church, so our bloody Prody friend gets a lovely view from their carriages as they pass by of their dead ones graves .Jayus, it's a joke."

John didn't answer in case, he said the wrong thing and lost this bit of work, a job was a job to him. When they got to the cemetery, the other men were waiting, hands in their pockets to keep themselves warm. Once the foreman arrived, who just happened to be the contractor's brother, there was no standing around.

"Hop to it, lads," he shouted, not missing a step, he continued to make his way to the other side of the graveyard. They made their way down to where the old granite stone church stood encircled by five oak trees. They were to climb the ladders and start digging out the mortar around the stone to loosen it. Then the pillars could be pulled down with ropes by the men on the ground. The first four pillars came down without any

---

[20]Mickey fit: slang :– to get mad
[21]Prody: slang for Protestant

problems, the last pillar near the belfry was proving to be stubborn; it was eight feet long and six feet wide; the stone itself was eighteen inches thick and was refusing to budge. John had worked on it for a good portion of the morning then Pat had a go at loosening the mortar. After a while, Pat descended the ladder and told the foreman that it was ready to be pulled down. The rest of the men were clearing stone on the ground, piling it up to be removed and rebuilt in another area of the grave yard.

John stared up at the pillar. "There's enough outta that now, for sure," he said.

The foreman: who had been in a foul mood all day shouted back that 'there wasn't enough mortar out of it'.

John rolled his eyes and sighed in defeat. "Might[22], lads. Might," John called to the men as Pat started to ascend the ladder again.

Suddenly, without warning, there came a crunching sound, and the stone started to slowly slip away. Pat called out, "Look out!"

Everything began to happen so fast that there was little time to react as the pillar started to shake. The men jumped out of the way as best they could. Pat jumped to safety hitting the ground hard, just in time to see John scrambling over stones that lay everywhere. Trying to get away, taking one last look up as he ran. Suddenly, a hail of rubble came tumbling down, causing the entire pillar to collapse. John still wasn't clear of the site, still struggling to get over the debris, when everything came crashing down on him, completely covering his whole body. The air was filled with dust, great thuds echoed all around them as the stone hit the ground and then started piling up on top of itself. Dazed, the men looked all around checking to see if everyone was safe.

---

[22]Might: old language not used any more, meaning "to use your strength"

Pat called, "Murray, where's Murray?"

The men realised that the rubble was covering him. They began frantically pulling the stone away by hand, with a strength they didn't know they had left in them. Slowly, they could see parts of his body as they dug deeper and faster. They pulled his arms free and yanked him out from under the remaining stone. It was clear to everyone right away that John was dead as he was covered in dust and mortar, blood seeping from a deep wound in his chest. They washed his face and tried listening for his breath, but there was none. John was only thirty-two years old when he died.

In disbelief and badly shaken, they slowly removed their caps and blessed themselves, kneeling to say the Lord's Prayer. One of the men ran to see if he could find a priest to say a few words. The Foreman sat with his head in his hands, trying to think of how he was going to get out of this mess. After a while, he walked quickly away to find the Director of the Cemetery to tell him what had happened. It was agreed that John's body would have to go to the morgue to determine the cause of death. The foreman returned to the men a little later who were all standing around gloomily. John's body had been covered in someone's jacket and the priest was talking to some of the men trying to find out what had happened.

On seeing this, the foreman raising his arms called to all of them, "Well, men, we all know this was a terrible accident. No one is to blame here. The wall was weak and Murray should have known that and got out of the way. So, no use blaming anyone, am I making myself clear?" He asked the assembled crowd.

They kept their heads down, some mumbled things unheard. But no one spoke up. Satisfied, the foreman instructed them to make some sort of stretcher to carry John's body. A horse and cart would be at the front of the cemetery to take John to the morgue. He called Pat aside.

"Pat, I believe you knew Murray better than most of us, so I'd be grateful if you could inform his wife as to his passing," he said rather business-like.

Pat couldn't believe his ears, so he was being sent to do their dirty work and stood open-mouthed for a minute. Then regaining his composure he nodded, slapping his hat off his leg as he set off. He knew the consequences if he didn't play along: he'd lose his job and he had a family to feed and they had to come first. Satisfied, the foreman simply walked away.

Pat walked through the streets of Dublin in despair. What would he say? How could he tell Mary that she was a widow, her son fatherless? With no one to support them, Patrick knew the future looked bleak. The accident kept playing over and over in his mind, with each step he took.. It played over as if in slow motion the blocks kept tumbling down. John's face floated before his eyes, dull and motionless. God he wished he hadn't gone to work today.

After John had left that morning, Mary had sat thinking. The room was quiet except for the soft sound of William breathing. Mary shook her head, scolding herself; she realised how unfair she was being to John. Her pain was also shared by him. But she hadn't been able to stop herself. Well, it stops today. From now on, she would make a better effort. John needed her too, she had reproached herself. She gently shook William awake, telling him to rise and get washed, handing him the water bucket to fill on his way back up.

She made him something to eat. When he returned, she repeated what his father had said he was to do, and sent him off to the market. She dressed herself and tidied the room. She would make a lovely stew for John. He deserved it. She promised Our

Lady she'd do better. Already she was feeling more hopeful. She had her John and she had William. She would be strong and not shut them out. She began to prepare the stew and then sat and sipped some tea and smoked a woodbine. She thought she heard a gentle knock on the door and stood to answer it. She stared puzzled. Patrick Fitzgerald stood before her, covered in dirt and sweat. She noticed he was shaking. "What tis it, Pat? Aren't ya workin' wit John today? Ye looks awful," She started to babble as if she already knew why he was there.

"Mary, Jayus, Mary, I don't know how to tell ya this," Pat spoke in a whisper, head down.

Suddenly, Mary felt panic rising in her throat.

"Ya wants tay[23], Pat?" She asked, turning away from him, trying to busy herself.

Pat grabbed her arm and turned her towards him. Her eyes were full of fear, her lips trembled, as she gently shook her head.

"Mary," Pat tried to say.

"Just say he's going to be grand," She begged.

Pat stood for a minute. "He's gone, Mary, I'm truly sorry," he said, choking on the words.

Mary felt her breathing momentarily stop, and then she started gasping for air. "Gone! Gone! What are ya talking about?" She spoke in gasps.

Pat blurted out that the stones had fallen on him; there was nothing any of them could do. It happened so fast.

"But why not you?. Why John? Why not one of the other men? It couldn't be John. Are ye sure it was him? Are ya?"She said as she tried desperately to process the information. Then she could hear someone screaming like a banshee[24], but she had no idea it was herself. She began pounding Pat's chest.

---

[23]Tay: Irish word for tea still used by people today in some places
[24]Banshee: Irish legend a female spirit wailing warns of a death in the house

"Why not you?. Why John?".

Pat tried to hold her. She struggled against him and then collapsed into his arms and continued to scream.

William was struggling up Mary's Lane with some pallets he had found at the market when he heard the soul-retching screams. The women washing their clothes in the yard stopped and looked up, blessing themselves. A scream like that could mean only one thing – someone had died. William, recognising the owner of the scream, dropped the pallets and started running.

As quick as lightning, raggy children emerged from every doorway to covet the discarded treasure of pallets.

Taking the stairs two at a time and falling in at the door breathless, he saw his ma screaming. A man he didn't recognise was holding her.

"What ya do to her? I'll kill ya, gits away from her! Just wait till me da gits hold of ya," He shouted at the man, fist raised.

They both turned and Mary reached out to hug William. "William! Oh! My God!, William!" Mary cried as she dragged a struggling William over to the bed.

William knew it must be bad, the only time he saw his mother like this was when the babies died. But there were no babies. So he was confused. Mary sat with him, staring into his eyes. John's eyes, she thought. William waited, breathless. But no matter how she tried, she just couldn't say the words. She looked up at Pat for help.

Pat knelt down beside them and told William what had happened. "Where's me da?" He asked Pat.

"In the morgue, son," Pat answered, not able to look at either of them. Mother and son hugged each other and cried.

At the age of twelve, William's world shattered into a million pieces.

John's Death Certificate

Extract from Evening Mail on Accident in Glasnevin Cemetery 1879

Can you Spare a Penny, Mister?

Some people possess an inner strength so strong it carries them through every hardship and sorrow that life can throw at them. Not only does it carry them, it carries those they love. For others, it is the strength of these people that keeps them strong and they are happy to be carried by it. For Mary, with John gone, the babies gone and only herself and William left, she could find no inner strength, for John had been hers.

John's body was to be buried in Glasnevin Cemetery the day after the coroner's report. There was no surprise when the coroner declared it an accident, even though it was quite clear that they had been ordered to go back up the ladder and remove more mortar. No one had been prepared to go up against the contractors in case they lost their jobs. They had their families to think about.

The evening before the burial, neighbours had called to pay their respects. In a small gesture of help, they brought with them a little oatmeal, a cup of buttermilk, a bowl of stew, or some turf, whatever they could spare. They were struggling to feed themselves, but still they shared what little they had. They understood Mary's grief and blessed themselves and thanked God it wasn't them, for how would Mary and William survive now?

The men that worked with John had collected a few shillings

amongst themselves; it would help Mary pay the rent that week. She had also received John's wages: which consisted of a quarter pound of tea, a loaf of bread and an ounce of butter. After that, it would be up to Mary to provide for them.

Like robots, Mary and William had continued to function. Their room where the wake was held was cramped and stuffy. Whiskey was drunk and memories shared, followed by rebel songs that continued long into the night.

Amidst all this, Mary had stood over the coffin set up on their little table, the same table they had all sat happily, every evening. She stared at the person lying there; it looked like John, except John was warm and loving, so full of life. He had always been able to make her laugh. This wasn't him. This empty shell wasn't John. She reached out and touched the scratches and bruises on his beautiful face. Her fingers traced the small scar on his left cheek, as she had done many times late at night in the darkness of their room. He lay like stone and her brain fought to make sense of what she was seeing. A small tear dropped on to his cheek and she had gently wiped it away. Finally, she bent down to kiss his marbled skin, recoiling from the icy cold. Then reaching out again, she stroked his hair, whispering, "Tis only you, John." She knew she would never again hear him say "Tis only you, Mary" as she stepped away.

When the sun rose, mother and son were wrapped up in John's old army coat and huddled together. The smell of John still lingered on his coat, and they inhaled deeply. Mary imagined she could still hear him breathing in and out lying beside her. Sleep evaded her.

Mary and William accompanied John's body in its white washed coffin, rosary beads placed on top. As they made their way to the cemetery, large dark clouds rolled across the sky. The heavens opened, sending heavy rain that mixed with their salty tears. They stood solemnly holding each other, staring into the huge hole which was his grave. Unknown to them, Julia, who'd died only one month previously, lay buried at the head of John in a similar pauper's grave.

A few prayers were said by an uncaring priest. Then the world carried on, not missing a beat for everyone but them.

As they wandered home, not a word was spoken. They climbed the stairs and got into bed, wrapped themselves up in John's coat, then quietly cried.

William had risen the next morning and prepared some food for Mary, but she made little effort to eat it. He then went out to the market to see if he could find any work; it was hardly worth the effort. His heart just wasn't in it. The downward looks from people, not wanting to make eye contact with him, people who had known his Da, just made him want to run and run and never stop. A sudden loud cackle of laughter from some customers going about their day grated on his nerves and sent his mind asking, *Why are they laughing? What would anyone have to laugh about?* A panic rising out of nowhere filled him. He ran back to the safety of their little room as quickly as he could. He lit the fire and looked at his mother.

"Ma, Ma," he asked, "Are ya getting up? Can ya get up now?" William pleaded.

Mary never responded. She lay in the bed covered in John's coat, she cried on and off uncontrollably, then would go deathly silent, hardly moving. Even when Mr Lynch, the landlord, called looking for the rent, she had never even lifted her head.

"Mrs Petit, me sympathies but da rent is due, and ifin ya can't pay then you and the lad will have to leave," he had said indifferently. William reached up to the shelf and counted out the money his dad's workmates had collected and threw it on the table and stood back. Mr Lynch cupped his hand around the money and nodded to William. "See ya next week." Tipping his hat, he left without a word of either kindness or malice.

As the days passed, the little room began to smell and was freezing cold. William had no idea what to do, he had collected an old pallet and chopped it up, but it hadn't lasted long. In sheer desperation, he wrenched his Da's coat away from his ma and quickly ran down to the pawn shop; he only got a few shillings but it brought him bread, lard and tea. Delighted, he arrived home. On opening the door, his ma rose from the bed and slapped him hard across the face.

"Ya had no business taking yer Da's coat," she had screamed demonically at him, eyes red and wide, hair sticking up at weird angles. Startled at her own outburst, she stared for a moment at William then slumped back into the bed, sobbing. William stood stunned, hardly believing that his ma had struck him, as she had never done so before. Gathering himself together, he made tea and bread as Mary mumbled, "No right, it was yer Da's, no right."

The next week, Mr Lynch returned to demand his rent. But there was nothing to collect; they had nothing. Finally, after William had pleaded with him, he agreed to take the table and their two wooden chairs as payment. As he left, he grabbed Mary's China teapot from the mantelpiece to seal the deal. William stood in the middle of the empty room as tears rolled down his face while Mary remained still and lifeless on the straw mattress.

Having run out of options, he made the decision to call down to Mrs Carey for help. She had taken one look at his tired and drained face and brought him in. She knew by the look of him that he hadn't eaten for days. Mrs Carey was getting on in years and couldn't make the stairs anymore, so she hadn't been able to go up and visit Mary.

She asked, "How's your Ma doing, lad?" As she passed him, a bowl of steaming hot stew and chunks of stale bread, putting them down in front of William.

"She's not too good, Mrs Carey," William replied through mouthfuls of food, "I don't know what to do. My Uncle Pat and Catherine have called round twice to give us some bread and tea, but say they can't do it no more because they don't have enough for themselves and me Ma should gits up and try and find work. But she's gone. She's just not here anymore and I don't know what to do."

Suddenly, his face crumbled and great sobs escaped his lips; his whole body shook and Mrs Carey wrapped her arms around him and cradled him close.

"Ya cry, lad, gits it out, all out, no point holding it in, it's just going to choke ya and make ya bitter. You're right to cry, yer r Da was a good man. May God be good to him," she said, cradling him until his tears were spent.

When he calmed down, his face was streaked with dirt, his eyes red and snots covered his nose and mouth. Taking a wet cloth, Mrs Carey washed his face.

"Come on now, eat dat drop of soup and I'll give ya some for yer ma, I can't make the stairs no more, my legs are too swollen or I'd have come round to see her. I'm so sorry, William, I can't do anything more than give ya some stew and bread." She sighed.

"Mrs Carey, I'm grateful, so grateful to ya, tank ya. I'll pray for ya."William gobbled up the stew, dunking the bread in it to soften it. He was so hungry he could hardly even taste it. When he finished, Mrs Carey gave him a Billy can with soup and had wrapped up some bread for Mary.

"Tanks, Mrs Carey, can I gits ya some coal or some water up from the backyard?"offered William.

"You're a good lad, young William, but me daughters gits it for me. Ya go on now and look after yer poor ma. Your ma needs ya now," said Mrs Carey .After William had left, carefully carrying the stew for his Ma, Mrs Carey made her way a little unsteady and stood by the statue of the Virgin Mary which was placed on her dresser. She prayed for the young lad and asked God to help him to be brave and strong at such a young age, she prayed for his mother that she would find the strength to look after her boy and herself.

William leaned over his mother."I've stew for ya, Ma, Mrs Carey gave it us. Sits up now and eat something. Will ya? Please, Ma!"

Mary stirred in the bed "William, what will we do? I don't know what to do; I just don't know what to do."Mary sobbed.

"Just eats, Ma," replied a weary William, climbing into bed beside her. "Just eat."

Every day, William was forced to leave his Ma lying in bed and he would go scouring the streets looking for work or wood or anything that would help the situation. Every day, things got more and more unbearable and the young lad was at a loss as to how to make it better. Returning to the tenements, the smells filtering from the other rooms of cooking nearly drove him mad.

William imagined it was cabbage and potatoes or even a bit of ham. His stomach turned over and bile rose up in his throat. He felt sick, he hadn't eaten since Mrs Carey had given him stew and that was days ago. He never remembered being this weak and hungry. So, before entering the little room, he turned on his heel and headed down the stairs once more, to Mrs Carey.

He stood hesitantly at the door and then timidly knocked. After a minute, the door swung open. Mrs Carey's daughter stood glaring down at him.

"So tis you, ya little rascal come back again, ya should be ashamed of yourself. Your ma has no pride, sending ya begging from an auld woman. How dare ya scrounge off me ma. If in I see ya around 'ere again, I'll box the ears off ya. I swear to you, I box the ears off ya," she screamed and threatened with her small fist shoved in his face.

William was dumbfounded and didn't know what to say, he was frightened and he could hear Mrs Carey in the background.

"Ah! Sure leave the lad alone, Lily, tis not his fault, don't be so un-Christian," she spoke meekly as if she wasn't well.

"Unchristian!" She shrieked. "Ifin I catch him around 'ere begging and scrounging off ya again, I'll feckin kill him. Now gits out here quick or I'll take a brush to ya," she yelled, reaching for the brush. "I feckin mean it." With that, she slammed the door so hard the walls vibrated.

William ran back up the stairs and sat on the landing. He cried, confused. What had he done wrong? Wasn't Mrs Carey a friend of his ma's? The hunger was too great to ignore and there was no point going back into his ma's.

Catherine had called round yesterday and tried to get Mary up out of bed and washed, but to no avail. His ma had cursed and screamed at Catherine to get out, until she had done just that. Sighing and throwing William a look of defeat, she had stormed out without a backwards glance. Now with nothing left to do, William pulled on his father's cap and headed for Sackville

Street[25] to try begging.

It was dangerous to beg; if the coppers caught you, they sent you to court and then away to some awful place. William knew this, but hunger had got the better of him. He called out to passer-by, "Can ya spare a penny, mister." He begged as he dodged in and out of the men walking past, avoiding any women. They stared down at him with contempt. They glared down at his dirty ragged clothes and his filthy face, his grubby fingernails and unkempt hair. They sidestepped him whenever they could, to avoid getting close to such a disgusting creature, afraid of catching something contagious. Some just looked past him as if he was invisible. After an hour, William sat by the bridge with his head in his hands, tears running down his face he whispered, *"Da why did ya leave us? Why, Da?"*

Suddenly, someone grabbed him by the collar and pulled him up to his feet and started yelling, "Well now! Boyo, begging, are you? You'll be sorry, ya little fecker. What's your name? Now don't try lying to me, I've got you now, boy," grinned the constable, all the while struggling to keep hold of him. William looked up into the constable's face, he twisted and struggled .He fought hard to get away but the constable was a big man and had a good hold of his collar with one hand and his left ear with the other.

"What's your name? What's your name now? There's no point trying to get away," he said, shaking him harder while pulling and pinching his ear.

"William, William Le Petit, sir, I haven't done nothing, sure I haven't, I'm just sitting 'ere," he pleaded.

"You've been begging, boyo, I seen ya, I've been watching

---

[25] Sackville Street: Renamed O'Connell Street in 1924 in honour of Daniel O'Connell, a nationalist leader

ya, and now you're going to pay, you're going somewhere that will teach ya a lesson. lazygood for nothing Irish. And you ain't coming back. Now tell me where you live, where is your ma? Where is your da?" He shouted at William.

"Me da is dead, this two weeks, he fell in Glasnevin Cemetery. Me ma she's in bed, she won't get up, I ain't done nothing," a frightened William replied.

"Where do you live?" the constable said, putting his face close to William's.

William had no choice but to tell him. William was marched along the streets still held by his ear, until they got to the tenements. Pounding and pounding on the door, it was eventually answered by a very bedraggled Mary. She stood staring at the constable and then at William, back at the constable and then at William not knowing what to make of the situation.

Pushing his way into the foul-smelling room, he inquired, "Are you the lad's mother?"

Mary took a moment to answer. Totally baffled, she said, "I am. What's da trouble?".

"Da trouble," he mimicked. "Your son's the trouble, caught begging on Sackville Street and I'm charging him. He's to appear in the District Court on Wednesday and let me tell you, Mrs Petit, it's more than likely that he'll end up in one of the institutions. Begging is a crime under section eleven of the law and the magistrate doesn't take too kindly to it. I'm Constable Ryan, meet me at the District Court on Wednesday at nine a.m. Best to pack his bags because he won't be coming home," he sneered, looking around the room.

"Bloody dirty, lazy Irish," he said as he threw William onto the mattress and left the stinking room, shooting Mary a disgusted look as he left.

The appearance of the constable jolted Mary into reality. She looked down at her dirty clothes then she looked at William who sat sobbing. He was filthy dirty, Mary hardly recognised him. She didn't recognise herself. Spurred into action, she grabbed the water bucket, pulling William up she ordered him to go down to the lane and get clean water. While he was gone, she tidied and straightened the bed; there was no turf left to light the fire. When William arrived with the water, she told him to wash and change his clothes.

"Stop your bloody cryin', boy, I don't know what ya done, but you've got to get your Uncle Pat. So gets cleaned up, here's your da's shirt. Ya better hope Pat knows what to do, William."

After William had washed and changed his clothes, she sent him again down to the yard to get more water and then she told him to fetch his Uncle Pat.

When he'd left, she washed herself and changed her clothes. She stared at the red petticoat lying on the floor. She remembered the morning she had shown Catherine the petticoat and said she would dye it red. Now it lay there faded and dirty. *Where had the girl who dreamed as she scrubbed the washing gone?* She wondered. Dismissing it, she busied herself, scouring the floor and changing the sheet on the bed that stank to high heaven. She worked with a flurry of energy as if cleaning would make the situation better. By the time she'd finished, Pat had arrived; William had already filled him in as to what had happened.

"I can't believe it, I just can't believe ya let dis happen. Why didn't ya get up out of the bed? Why didn't ya try?" asked a bewildered Patrick.

"I don't know why I didn't try. I guess it was cos me husband up and died. Don't start blaming me Pat, I couldn't help me, so how could I help him?" She said, pointing at William. "What are we going to do? What are we going to do?" She began crying and panicking. "I can't lose William too, I just can't lose William. What am I going to do? What can we do? Is there anything we can do? Pat, help me! Mother of Jayus, please help me," she pleaded, totally hysterical.

Patrick calmly sat down on the bed, his head down. He had enough problems of his own and he was already getting tired of carrying Mary.

"Tis nothing we can do. I'm sorry. But ifin ya look at it dis way, Mary, the lad needs a trade, tis his only chance, he'll get dat in an industrial school. Ye can't go on like dis. I can't keep ya and William. Look at him, Mary, tis not right. Anyway, it's out of our hands, da court will send him away, Mary, make no mistake about dat. Mary, please listen!"

But Mary refused to listen. "No, I'll talk to the judge, tell him it was just a mistake, they'll surely listen. The lad's da has just died," she counselled herself.

Patrick sighed. "Surely ye know by now, Mary, they don't care about the likes of us. The lad will go and you've only yourself to blame; it was your place to look after him when John died and ya didn't. No judge is going to listen to ya."

He looked at William sitting sadly on the mattress. His heart went out to him, but it was out of their hands now and on Wednesday, William would surely start a different life. As far as Patrick was concerned, it was the best thing that could happen, as Mary just couldn't cope.

Mary looked up, furious. "How dare ya. How dare ya. I asked ya ere to help us, not call me a bad ma. I luvs me son. I luvs him, I loved John, don't say I'm a bad ma, Patrick, I couldn't help it .I just couldn't help it," she screamed at him.

"Mary, listen to me. I'm not atall saying you're a bad ma,

not atall. I'm just saying tis the way it's going to be, ye need to come to terms with it by Wednesday, git used to the idea and I'll be standing right beside ya, as I always done. But if in ya tink about it, he'll get a trade and he'll be able to have a good life and dat's what ya want for him and dat's what John would want for him. Now git ye selves some food," he said handing her some bread and a little tea. "Try and sleep and I'll see ya on Wednesday outside the court house. Make sure ye are clean and are on time," he said as he left them to ponder on what would happen on Wednesday.

The days dragged on, neither knew what to say to the other. It would take every ounce of strength Mary had left to get through the next few days, she had to be strong and fight for William. Yes, she would explain to the judge it was all a mistake and they would go home and carry on with their lives. So she washed their few items of clothes and made William bathe and they waited for the dreaded Wednesday to come. Each lost in their own painful thoughts. A sense of foreboding hung over them. Mary felt like she was spiralling off a cliff. She questioned, why had God taken John and left them like this?

Fate was about to step in once more and change their lives forever.

By the time Wednesday arrived, Mary was numb with fear. William had hardly spoken and neither had slept. Not having a shilling to pay a knocker – up [26] to wake them, they listened for the church bells of St Michin's to ring out so they ould gauge the time. They arrived outside the courthouse just before nine. Patrick and Catherine were waiting for them, a little annoyed that

---

[26]Knocker up: a professional who wakes people up at a designated time for an agreed fee.

they had only just made it in time. The foursome proceeded into the large room where the magistrate perched on the high platform towered above them. They were to wait until his name was called and William was to stand up in the dock and the magistrate would proceed with the sentence. It was a done deal, begging was not acceptable, no matter what the circumstances. After a long wait, the clerk called out, "William Le Petit." Nervously, William walked to the dock and stood beside Constable Ryan, shaking. He looked what he was: a small frightened boy.

The clerk stood up and called out, "Case number 1495, Magistrate Albert O'Dowd preceding."

The magistrate sat with his dirty grey wig plopped on top of his balding head. Behind him on the wall was the Royal Coat of Arms painted with gold leaf. A British flag stood to the right side of him. William peered around, taking everything in until Constable Ryan gave him a dig in the ribs, forcing him to keep his eyes down or get another dig. Then he proceeded to read out the charge of begging on Sackville Street on 21stApril 1879, in the year of Her Majesty Queen Victoria's reign.

The Magistrate looked bored; yet another dull, petty, Irish case. How he longed to be proceeding over an exciting case in the Circuit Court. But he was stuck here with the ignorant, lazy, dirty Irish and he was weary and fed up with it.

"Yes, yes," he said irritably. "Yes, four years' incarceration at St Joseph's Industrial School[27] should do him some good," he ordered.

Mary sat listening in the gallery, wringing her hands over and over. Suddenly, she heard four years, St Joseph's Industrial

---

[27]St Joseph's Industrial School: later known as Artane Industrial School. Run by the Christian brothers. Known for its harsh and brutal treatment of children in their care. Open from 1870–1969 to take in the homeless/parentless poor children. Or for committing petty crimes

School. William and Mary's eyes met for a painful moment. Before she knew it, she was shouting, "Sir! your Majesty! Me lord! Your honour! Please can ya hear me? Please can I speak? Can I speak for me son?" she called, trying everything to get his attention. She tried to make her way to the front of the courtroom.

The magistrate, highly annoyed at the outburst, brought his hammer down hard several times. "Order!, order."

Mary wasn't listening, she was panicking. "Sir, please. Please can ya hear me? My husband just died and the boy wasn't begging. Tis all a mistake, I promise ya, on the blessed virgin. It was all a mistake," she pleaded, and begged in desperation. "I'll do better, sir, swear to god I will."

"Madam, if you do not be quiet, I will have you removed from the court immediately! Are you trying to say that Constable Ryan is lying?" he asked her, pointing to Constable Ryan.

"Not at tall, sir," she replied nervously. "It's just, tis a mistake and the boy, he done nothing wrong."

The magistrate stared at her for a moment in utter contempt.

"Madam is that a ring I see on your finger?" He asked, squinting down at her.

Mary, a little baffled, looked down at the bronze ring that John had given her on their wedding day. "It tis, Sir. Tis me wedding ring."

"And can you eat a wedding ring?" The judge laughed and looked at the ushers for support, who joined in with the laughter. Mary pursed her lips, staring at them all with pure hatred.

"Well, madam you could have fed your son and paid your rent had you sold that ring," he scolded her.

Shaking her head, not understanding what he was trying to say, she answered, "Sir, I couldn't be selling me wedding ring. My husband gave it me. Tis all I have left of him. How could I sell me wedding ring?" She asked in disbelief.

"Madam, you failed to look after your son and now he will go to an industrial school for a minimum of four years[28]. He'll learn a trade and have the care you should have given him. May I add, Mrs Petit, had you looked after your son, you would not be in this situation. You have no one to blame but yourself." He looked down into her face and signed the document that would seal William's future.

Unexpectedly, Mary started screaming and crying. Pat tried to hold her, but she had the strength of a tiger in that moment trying to get to her cub. She began to climb over the pews that were in her way, hindered by her long skirt and by Patrick who was holding her by the waist. "Mary, stop, don't make it any worse!" Patrick tried to plead with her.

"Remove that woman immediately," cried the magistrate, not looking up.

She kicked out at the constables who grabbed her, trying to remove her from the courtroom. She squirmed and twisted, desperate to get away and over to William. "William, William," she screamed. Her cries rang out around the courtroom.

William listened to the screams of his mother as she was dragged away. He tried desperately to get a glimpse of her. But a firm grip was kept on his shoulder. Everyone was in the way, and he was too small to see. He felt helpless to do anything and he wondered if he would ever see his ma again.

Without a word, he was pulled away by Constable Ryan who would accompany him on his journey to St Joseph's to start his time.

---

[28] If children were orphans or had been homeless. if parents were incapable of looking after their children, the court had the right to send them to an Industrial school.

All the while, Catherine had stood at the back of the courtroom watching the spectacle unfold. Images of the past flashed before her eyes. Times where she had felt so envious of Mary, her loving husband, her children. How happy and united her and John had been, how blessed to have children, when she had none. Patrick was a good husband, but not romantic and not as openly loving. She had often looked on wishing she were Mary. Now as Mary screamed and cried, she could only feel pity for her long-time friend. How blessed she was not to be Mary.

St Joseph's Industrial School

It wasn't a long journey, as William stared out of the barred window in dismay. Before he knew it, there were miles and miles of fields and nothing else. Eventually, a huge foreboding building appeared on the horizon. It was perched in the middle of fields and surrounded by a high wall. William's heart pumped hard, as the police wagon swung into the long driveway and up to the front door. Before getting out, Constable Ryan turned to William.

"If I can give you any advice, young lad, it's this, do what the brothers say. Work hard, keep your head down and you'll come out the other side a better man." And with that, he alighted from the wagon. Holding onto William by his collar, he knocked with the large brass knocker attached to the front door.

A man in a long brown robe answered the door, nodded to the constable and took William in. He never said a word; he just walked with him down the longest corridor William had ever seen. On and on as long as any street William knew. Eventually, they came to a huge heavy door. The brother knocked and William was ushered in. Brother Joseph sat behind a highly polished mahogany desk; his glasses perched at the very tip of his nose. He continued writing as William entered and stood in front of him. After what seemed like an eternity, he looked up.

"William Le Petit," he said staring at William. William didn't know what to do. "Boy! I said William Le Petit." He spat as he addressed William.

"'Yes, sir," William answered hesitantly, his body shaking.

"I'm Brother Joseph, the head brother here. If you're ever sent to me, then you know you are in serious trouble. So don't let me see you up here. Do you understand me? And you will address all of us as brother." William nodded.

"Yes brother," William answered.

Then Brother Joseph began by asking all kinds of questions. Was he Catholic? Where was his mother? Where was his father? What age was he? Could he read and write? Then he looked at his eyes and noted the colour. He noted his height and then he rang a bell. The brother had been waiting outside the door.

"Brother Mark, show William to the dormitories, get him washed and disinfected. He'll start class tomorrow. Thank you, Brother Mark." He looked directly at William and said, "William, you're here for a long time. If it's a good time, that's up to you." William was then ushered out of the room.

William was taken to what was a very primitive shower. But he'd never seen a shower before, so to him it seemed amazing not to have to wash in a trough outside as he'd done at home. He was given disinfectant to wash his hair and body. Brother Mark stood nearby watching, running his tongue over his bottom lip. William was embarrassed and turned his back to hide his privates. The disinfectant burned his skin and made it red and itchy. But William would not cry. He was given clean clothes which weren't much better than the rags that he had just taken off. A patched green shirt and brown trousers made of rough tweed and a pair of hobnail boots. The clothes had a strange smell to them, but at least they were clean. Brother Mark then brought him down to a large refectory hall, where there were hundreds of boys who sat line after line at wooden tables on wooden benches, eating some sort of porridge. The brothers sat at the top of the room high on a raised wooden platform. Here they could keep an eye on the boys and make sure there was no talking. A very sad-looking Jesus hung from a cross behind them. William was ushered to a table. This was the first time that William realised he hadn't eaten anything in days and he was hungry. He wasn't sure what it was in the bowl before him. Still he reached for his spoon just as a brother passed him and was immediately boxed in the ears. "Prayers first boy."

William was stunned into silence; his father had never raised his voice to him, let alone struck him. The brothers proceeded to say prayers that lasted ten–fifteen minutes, by the time they could eat their porridge. It was stone cold, while the brothers' meal was not served until they had finished their prayers. The porridge sat in his stomach all day, like a heavy lead brick just waiting to come back up.

William longed to be alone, so he could shed the tears that were stinging the back of his eyes. But he knew enough to know that this was not the place to cry. Brother Mark brought him around and showed him the school. Being only twelve, he would spend the next two years at school learning to read and write and arithmetic's and, of course, religious instruction was part of the curriculum. There were trade shops and a farm where the boys would be assigned a trade, but not until they were fourteen. He was surprised to learn that they played Gaelic football under the supervision of Brother Seamus. He had never learned to play football; he had just kicked around a hardened ball made of various rags. He thought that he might actually enjoy that. But nothing was fun here; this place was run by a regimented and harsh regime. Where there were frequent corporal punishments for any and every infraction, as the brothers liked to say," It is better to punish the body, and save the soul".

Later, he was brought to the dormitory. Rows of metal beds

stood in a line on either side of the room. Fifteen boys shared one dormitory. They took turns of five boys at a time to take a wash in the indoor bathroom, something that was new to William but the freezing water was the same as the yard at home. Brother Mark stood in the bathroom, while the boys washed to make sure they washed their hands and face and behind their ears and then they put on their nightshirts and were told to stand at the end of their beds to say the evening prayer. After that, it was lights out.

"There is to be no talking or there would be a severe punishment," Brother Mark had informed him, rubbing the leather strap that hung from his waist. William didn't want to talk. Neither could he sleep. He had spent most of the day in a frozen state of fear. All he could do was wonder how his mother was? How did he get here? How could he make his stay here better? then, he silently cried and cried. He had never felt so utterly alone and afraid in all his life.

One day was the same as the last; you got up, you got washed, you got dressed, you went down to the refectory. Prayers were said, you ate what looked like mush, and sometimes you didn't know what it was supposed to be. Then you went to the school that was Brother Aloysius' territory. He was mainly kind, even at times patient. William remembered small bits of what he'd learned from his father, but the arithmetic's went right over his head and earned him many a pinched ear or a punch. Every day, there were two hours of physical education. It was conducted like a military operation. They did squats, running on the spot, chest out, shoulders back, into scissor jumps. They had to climb a rope that hung from the ceiling, all the while Brother Seamus screamed at them, "Harder, faster, quicker, you're idiots! You're lazy! You're stupid. Healthy body, healthy mind, boys," he'd say as he tapped his cane on the floor in rhythm. Three times a week

,they were taken swimming, where you either swam or you drowned. Sometimes, the brother held you under the water for what seemed like an eternity for no particular reason. So you learned to swim pretty quickly after that.

There were, of course, religious instructions which seemed to take up a lot of the classes. There were prayers for morning, afternoon, evening and bedtime and for punishments.

Amongst all this were children known as the bastards (it was better to be known as an orphan than to be a bastard). The brothers made no secret of their hatred towards the bastards and they got it worse than other boys; " the sins of the father shall be visited on the son"[29]. Or in their case, the sins of the mother were taken out on the bastards. Their mothers were called whores, fallen women; the boys were told that no one, not even God, forgave a whore. The children were also told that they too weren't wanted, not by these fallen women or any family member. They were there out of the kindness of the brothers' hearts and they had damn well better not forget that. Because if they hadn't come here. They would be on the streets. Tarving to death. Or wrapped in a bundle and thrown into the river Liffey. Be sure that no God-fearing Catholic would bury a bastard.

William was neither so he didn't know where he fit in, but this would change in time.

Some boys would be quite excited when it came to Sundays, then their parents would be able to come and visit them and maybe bring them a treat, which the brothers quickly confiscated after the parents had left. William had been told that his mother would not be allowed to visit him for two months to allow him to adjust to his new life. Every Sunday when the two months had passed, he would sit very excited in the long hall, on a high

---

[29]taken from book of Exodus 20:5

wooden chair, his legs dangling off the ground. Here, he waited to be called to see his mother. He would look forward to this all week; it was what kept him going. He couldn't wait to hug his ma, he missed her so much.

But she never came, and every Sunday as Brother Mark escorted him back to the dormitory, he would ask the same question with mocked surprise, "What, your mother never came! Again?"

A couple of months later, Brother Joseph, with a hint of glee, told him that his mother had died. "You had better just get on with it, no crying would be tolerated. She is gone, no loss there, for really what had she done for you, boy?" he had asked, staring directly at William, waiting for him to confirm that his mother was not worth his tears.

"Nothing, brother," mumbled William.

Brother Joseph smiled pleased to see that William wouldn't give him any trouble. And that was that, he was an orphan now. That is how he was told, no kind word, no hug, no sympathy, nothing, just matter of fact, and get on with it. William couldn't believe his mother had died. He was given no reason for her death. No time, no place, nothing. He grieved inwardly, not wanting the bullies to see his weakness. At night, he could hear her calling him, "William, William, William", as she had done in the courtroom that fateful day. The brothers assured him that she hadn't even tried to visit him; she cared so little about him. She had left him too, Da had also gone and now, there was only William.

This heralded a very bad period for William. The anger inside had to find a way out and it did, in the form of fighting. William's main companion was O'Malley with the gunner eye[30].

---

[30]Gunner eye: eye that is crooked or turned inwards

O'Malley was one of the bastards. But he slept in the bed beside William and they soon became friends. O'Malley would go on in life to fight in the 1916 rising[31] and be sent to a British jail for his participation in the battle. But for now, he was just a raggy boy like everyone else. Unfortunately, for O'Malley, because of his gunner eye, he became the brunt of everyone's joke, even the brothers thought it was funny to ask O'Malley, 'Why did he never look at them when they spoke to him?', and then slap him for not looking straight at them. With all the anger that William had built up, he became O'Malley's champion, he had grown protective of him. If O'Malley found himself in bother, William was there to defend him. And O'Malley was always in trouble. The more William fought the more beatings the brothers gave him. But nothing seemed to stop him. He was like a time bomb waiting to go off. O'Malley was delighted to have someone take up his cause. But sometimes it made things worse, because the bigger boys just wanted a chance to fight William.

William wasn't a particularly big child. He was quite scrawny and not very tall. But he could throw a punch. If there was a fight to be had, William was there.

One boy, O'Donovan, took particular delight at picking on O'Malley. On one particular morning, he had poured water on his mattress so it looked like O'Malley had pissed the bed resulting in a beating from Brother Mark, who then made O'Malley wash the sheet and stand outside in the cold with it over his head until it dried. Later, O'Donovan continued the humiliation at dinner by pulling his chair from underneath him, sending him crashing to the floor whereupon O'Donovan then stole his food. O'Malley tried hard to hide the tears, but he had had enough for one day

---

[31] 1916 rising: Irish Republican Brotherhood and volunteers, all across Ireland rose up against the British establishment

and the tears came anyway and this made the situation worse. O'Donovan laughed and taunted O'Malley, until William stepped in.

William waited until they were in the dormitory bathroom and then he shoved O'Donovan up against the sink and started pounding him with his fist. The boys all cheered and hollered, making a terrible racket. William kept pounding O'Donovan over and over until his anger was spent. William stood over his opponent with teeth and fists clenched breathing and grunting heavily. Blood and sweat ran down his face and his eye felt bruised and swollen from where O'Donovan had tried to fight back. The sounds in the dormitory were blocked out by the sheer anger he felt inside his head. As his temper subsided he looked down, and he suddenly realised that the object of his anger was not the raggy boy who lay beneath him but the mother who had abandoned him. The uncle that had betrayed him. and the father who had left him all alone. He looked at the battered and bruised boy who was just like him and felt ashamed. Blinking away the sweat, he stared, confused. All his anger had been channelled into a fight, any fight. Pausing for a moment, it dawned on him; it wasn't the boy he was angry with. He reached his hand down to the boy, who shrunk away thinking he was going to get another beating. William grabbed his hand and pulled him up and shook his hand. The boys cheered.

Out of nowhere, Brother Mark appeared; he grabbed William's arm and smashed him against the wall, punching him in the face, before dragging him to spend the night in the small cupboard. The brothers had later punished him severely. He had been beaten with the leather strap, so badly that he spent the next week in the infirmary, but this gave William time to reflect on his life so far. He was determined to get out of this place as fast as he could. If that meant being an exemplary pupil, then that is what he would be. He vowed that he would never fight in anger again.

When he eventually returned to the dormitory, O'Malley was nowhere to be seen and no one seemed to know where he went. William thought maybe he'd been moved to another school. But if anyone knew, no-one was saying. This left William to concentrate on himself. Nearly fourteen, he would be leaving school and going to the workshop to learn a trade. William fancied working on the farm. He imagined it would be peaceful and less confrontational. He didn't mind getting his hands dirty or working, anything to escape the classroom. The brothers, however, had other ideas. As soon as William returned from the infirmary, he was sent to the trade workshop and they chose shoemaker for his trade, much to William's disappointment. But it did mean he would be leaving school early. He had no choice anyway, so once again he conformed and settled into learning his trade. It was hard on his tender young hands, causing blisters all over his fingers that bled constantly, until they hardened up. He soon got the hang of it and even excelled at his given trade.

Mr Joyce, a layman, was the shoemaker over the boys and he was both patient and compassionate. He took pride in teaching them, their success was his success so he ensured the boys would eventually leave with all the skills they needed in their life outside of this place.

The atmosphere in the workshop was more relaxed and William slowly came out of his shell and started to enjoy the work and learned quickly, he had a dry sense of humour and was very likeable and fitted in well with the other lads. Having an easy-going personality helped him to avoid confrontation. If he felt his temper rising, he told himself, *'Keep your head down and get the hell out of here.'* For the best part, it worked well for him. So he soon settled.

Every evening, they had to return to their dormitories. William found this part hard. Returning to the brothers and their strict regime every night was like living in a nightmare. They constantly tried to break the boys' spirit. But the knowledge that he could escape each morning to the workshop was what carried him through the next two years. Mr Joyce was a keen Gaelic football fan and encouraged the boys to continue playing. He often arranged matches for them which were held on a Sunday. The whole school would come out and watch and cheer them on. William had enjoyed learning the game and was happy to play. Again, it was the smallest sense of normality that helped to heal him and kept him going. Mr Joyce somehow had managed to get the brothers to agree to let the boys play against St Mary's boys from the inner city, and a big game was arranged. The boys were very excited. Mr Joyce coached them and gave them confidence that they could win. A lot depended on the game as the whole school would attend, including the brothers. So if they failed, the brothers would most definitely put a stop to their Sunday training and probably punish them for letting the school down. But Mr Joyce had every confidence in them, even if they didn't.

On the day of the game, everyone was excited. They had no football shorts or tops, so they would play in their everyday clothes, but that didn't matter to them, they were playing football and not because they were forced to but because they wanted to. When the other team arrived fully kitted out in their parish Church's colours, there was a bit of hostility between them. The city boys looked down on the institution boys, with their shaved heads, bruised eyes and scaly legs as inferior beings. But nothing could dampen their high spirits, not even Brother Mark who had lined them up and had made it quite clear that they had better win.

"Remember, boys, this was the game of our ancestors, so play with pride." He would be watching. So if any boy dishonoured the game by playing dirty, he would deal with them severely, he had warned them. Out on the pitch, the boys tried hard to do their best, not for the brothers, but for Mr Joyce and for themselves. They didn't quite win. They only lost by a penalty. But the whole school cheeredevery time they got possession of the ball or scored a goal.

"You should feel proud of yourselves, boys; your first game and you played brilliantly, no shame here,"Mr Joyce had told them afterwards as he handed each boy an apple and a cordial[32]drink. Brother Mark on the other hand looked like thunder and asked to speak to Mr Joyce in his office as soon as the boys were finished.

Mr Joyce told the boys not to worry; he would smooth things over with Brother Mark.

It was at this point that a boy from the other team called out, "Petit, is that you, Petit?"

William looked around and he recognised a boy he had known from the lane: Danny Foley.

"Jayus, Petit, I taught it was ye. So this is where ya ended up. None of us had a clue where you'd been sent. I was truly sorry to ear what happened to ya and then your poor ma," he gushed, surprised and delighted to see William.

"Me ma? What do ya mean? What happened to me ma?" a bewildered William asked Danny, standing up close to his face.

"Don't ye know?" Danny asked.

"They didn't tell me anything, Danny. They control

---

[32]Cordial drink: flavoured juice made with fruit, water and sugar.

everything we do and say," William whispered. Looking over his shoulder, he saw that they had caught Brother Mark's attention. He reached out and shook Danny's hand as if congratulating him on the win.

"Tell us quickly, I have to go or he'll beat the living daylights out of me," said William hurriedly.

"I don't know much, yer ma was in a bad way when ye got sent away. What with yer da dying and all. She was drinking a lot and was sleeping in the halls of the tenements. She had no money for da rent. Swear to God everyone tried to help her. But then, we hears she gone to da workhouse, dat's all I know swear to ya," said Danny in a rush.

"Is she dead, Danny?" William quickly asked. He could see Brother Mark making his way over to them.

"Danny, tell me quickly," William pleaded.

"I—"Danny started to say then Brother Mark was upon them.

"Break it up, boys. You, lad, get back to your own team. William, you get inside now," he ordered, as he smacked him across the head.

Danny looked back at William as he walked away and shrugged his shoulders. He didn't have to say anything; William knew they had lied about his ma. William had plenty of time to digest this piece of information. Questions tumbled around his head, he was confused and angry. He knew the brothers had lied to him but couldn't work out why? If she was alive, why didn't she come to see him? Why had she abandoned him yet again? He tossed and turned at night. He could see her in the court; he could see her after his da had died. Nothing made sense.

Mr Joyce soon noticed a change in William and had confronted him.

"William, is there anything wrong, you don't seem like yourself just lately?'" he asked kindly. But William had just shrugged his shoulders and said he was grand.

"Just trying to get me work done," he replied, keeping his head down. He had learned long ago to keep his feelings to himself and that is what he did.

He grew bitter and angry towards his mother. He saw her as weak and selfish and that wouldn't be him. He would be strong. His inability to understand her actions and his unwillingness to forgive would leave a deep and lasting scar, one that would remain with him throughout his life. He vowed that he would survive this place and forget about the past for that is where those memories belonged; in the past. He would never mention his mother to anyone ever.

Six months left, William couldn't believe that in just six months he would be free of this hateful place, free of the brothers, free to start a new life. He had come a long way. Mr Joyce had been impressed with his natural talent for shoemaking. He was way ahead of the other boys, always asking Mr Joyce to show him more and more. Tthen with determination his head went down until he had mastered it. His efforts had not gone unnoticed by the brothers either. Early in May 1883, he was summoned to Brother Joseph's office. He was sixteen and a half and freedom was beckoning.

It happened just after breakfast as he made his way to the trade shop. Brother Mark pulled him aside and had told him he was to go directly to Brother Joseph's office. William's heart pounded. He couldn't think what he had done and feared the worst as he made his way down that long, long corridor to Brother Joseph's office. His legs were shaking and it was taking every ounce of strength to stop his knees from giving way from under him. He hesitated when he reached Brother Joseph's office then he timidly knocked.

"Come in," called Brother Joseph.

Brother Joseph sat with his head down as usual, not looking up. Finally, he finished what he was writing. William stood at his desk waiting patiently, his heart pounding, He couldn't imagine what was wrong, he couldn't remember doing anything. A fear rose up into his throat.

"William," Brother Joseph said, "I have good news; we have managed to secure you a position with Mr Shaw, a shoemaker. Well, he actually has a company and makes orthopaedic shoes and is willing to offer you a position, as you are now a licensed shoemaker." Brother Joseph showed no emotion. William would leave, he would go to Shaw's factory and work and that's that. William stood disbelieving

"But, brother, I'm not finished with my apprenticeship yet," he said, bewildered.

"Mr Joyce assures me that you are more than capable and have earned your licence and that this would be a great opportunity for you. So I have no reason to argue with Mr Joyce. After all, he's the one who trained you. Now Mr Shaw lives in Skerries and you will be leaving on Saturday to join his shoe company. Have you any questions, William?" Brother Joseph asked.

William had a million questions. He could not believe this was happening, that he would be leaving this dreadful place. How could this be true? God bless Mr Joyce, he must have put a word in for him. Where the hell was Skerries? William never asked any questions. All he heard was that he would be leaving and he was more than ready to go.

As he left the office, he passed a small boy sitting on a chair just outside. He had no shoes and his face was streaked with tears. William stared at him remembering his first encounter with the brothers. This boy was obviously coming into the institution. He wore his own clothes and not that of the institution. William wondered what had happened to bring him here and his heart went out to him. He could be only eight years old. He knew, even if the child didn't, that he had many hard years ahead of him. So William winked at him to reassure him as he passed. There was nothing else he could do for him; his fate lay in the lap of the gods. The small boy just gave a weak smile as William walked away; glad his time was at an end and not just beginning.

On Saturday morning, accompanied by Brother Mark, he was escorted to Amiens Street[33] train station. He had a small bag with him. There wasn't much in it, just another shirt, a pair of socks, a toothbrush and a hairbrush. The clothes he stood up in were all he had. William was excited and fearful all at once. There hadn't been any long sad goodbyes. He had few friends, as he had learned it was better to keep yourself to yourself.

But he did thank Mr Joyce for his help and kindness. Mr Joyce had shook his hand warmly and wished him well and with that William had left St Joseph's behind him.

He tried to absorb everything that he saw when they got to Dublin. He'd been so confined and so restricted in the institution that his senses were overwhelmed. Dublin was busy with people going about their business. William hadn't had this much stimulation in years and, 'women', he hadn't seen a woman, not since he last saw his ma in the courtroom. The smells and the

---

[33] Amiens Street was formerly the name of the train station now known as Connolly Station. Named after the socialist James Connolly for his part in the 1916 rising

sights were overpowering and his head reeled. He had never been on a train before and he wondered how he would know when it was time to get off, at this 'Skerries.' Sensing this, Brother Mark assured him that the conductor would walk through the carriages and tell him what the next station was and he was to listen for the word Skerries and get out there. He would meet a Mr Shaw. Mr Shaw had also arranged for some living accommodation with a widow, there he would get food and board.

"So remember your manners and be very respectful to her," Brother Mark had instructed.

William just wanted to be rid of the brothers for good. Neither spoke another word as they stood waiting for the train to get ready to leave. After a while, Brother Mark walked him along the platform so he could board the train, which stood, smoke billowing from its funnel. Passengers slowly began to board.

Brother Mark turned to William and said, "This is your train, remember now to listen out for the station 'Skerries' when the conductor calls it. Be a good man, William, for that's what you are now. You have a trade and that should carry you through your life. I hope that you've learned a lot during your time at the institution and that you will remember us in your prayers. Remember too how good the Christian brothers were to you and try to live a good Christian life," Brother Mark solemnly said, blessing him. He stood staring down at William, waiting for William to say something. Thank you! You were great! Thank you for saving my soul. Something! William suddenly turned and stepped up onto the train.

Brother Mark called to him, "William, have you nothing to say? Have you no words of gratitude for all the brothers have done for you?"

It was William's turn to stare down. He stood for a moment

and thought. He remembered the beatings, the humiliations, the punishments, the lies. The train started to choke and gently rock and slowly began to move. The conductor called, "All aboard", as he walked along, slamming the carriage doors shut. William quickly pulled down the window.

"Yeah, brother, I do have something to say."

Brother Mark smiled and stood taller, waiting for the praise he felt he deserved.

"Ya can kiss me arse, brother, that's what yous feckers can do. You's shower of bastards!," shouted William in triumph.

Brother Mark looked like he would have a heart attack. He gulped and went red in the face. He didn't know what to do. He couldn't reach William to thump him as he wanted to. Instead, he stood gobsmacked. No one had ever spoken to him like that before. He longed to grab William and pull him from the train. But the train was already on its way and William tipped his cap laughing, he shouted, "See ya, brother."

All Brother Mark could do was stand and glare at the departing train. *Beware, young William,* thought Brother Mark. *For revenge is a dish best served cold.*

William plopped down into one of the carriage seats laughing as the train chugged out of the station. He gently rocked in his seat with the rhythm of the train. It then dawned on him that maybe he would be in trouble when he got to the other station and that the brothers would come after him. *If that's the case,* thought William, *I'll run away, as some boys at the institution had done.* William chose to forget that they had been caught and brought back, had their heads shaved and were given a terrible beating. *They won't find me*, thought William confidently. *I'll go to the Americas or somewhere, but I'll never go back there.*

A young man sat across from him and smiled at William. He

had heard what William had said to the brother. But for whatever reason, he said nothing. Maybe he had suffered at the hands of the brothers also. William tipped his cap. "Grand Day," he said with a cheeky grin. And then using his best grammar he asked. "Sir, would you have a spare cigarette by any chance?"

The young man smiled again and handed him a pack of woodbines and some matches.

"Thank you, sir," nodded William, enjoying his first taste of freedom. He struck a match and lit a cigarette. He drew deeply on it and relaxed back into his seat, closing his eyes in pure pleasure. He tossed the pack and the matches back to the man who caught them with one hand.

"Where are you heading, son?" the man asked. The word 'son' stabbed William in the heart. He hadn't been called that since his father had died, and he swallowed hard and struggled to compose himself. He looked out of the window as the countryside whirled by.

After a minute, he gathered himself together and answered "Somewhere new, I'm starting an adventure," he said confidently and settled back to enjoy the ride.

William's entry into St Joseph's industrial school

Skerries, May 1883

Stepping off the train in Skerries, a sleepy fishing village, William took a deep breath. Fresh salty air filled his lungs. He shivered a little. It was colder here than in Dublin and he had no overcoat. On the journey down from Dublin, he determined that this was a new start for him. The harrowing and grief-stricken days of St Joseph's were behind him and amazingly there was still a human being inside him that wanted to live and be loved. At nearly seventeen, he would start his life again. The brothers had done a good job at separating any positive feelings he had for his mother into negative ones. But that was the past. From this day on, he would start a new life for himself. He was a licensed shoemaker now and master of his own destiny.

He looked along the platform, he was to meet Mr Shaw; apparently he owned a shoe and boot factory and had offered him work. He had his papers and letter of recommendation tucked safely in his pocket. Mr Shaw would also introduce him to Mrs Higgins who had kindly agreed (for a small price) to board him, while he worked for Mr Shaw. A tall thin man approached him; he had been watching out for William.

"William, is it?" he asked, stretching out his hand to shake William's. "I'm Thomas Shaw; I've been waiting for you. The brothers have said good things about you." He smiled.

William nodded in response and was pleased that Mr Shaw seemed friendly. They walked over to a tired old horse and cart and Mr Shaw hopped on board. William hadn't sat on top of a horse and cart before, only at the back of the tail gate so he was a little nervous. He quickly scrambled on top as Mr Shaw jerked the reins.

"On, Nelly, On," he called to the old horse. William hadn't quite settled in his seat and nearly tumbled back out, as the cart jerked forward.

Mr Shaw laughed. "Hold on tight, young lad, Nelly here races along at a terrific pace."

He chuckled, pleased at his own joke, as Nelly slowly trotted along barely moving at a walking pace. William smiled to himself; he was going to like this Mr Shaw.

It was a short ride from the station into Skerries. A small fishing village, where everyone knew everyone and a new face caused heads to turn. Mr Shaw just kept going until he got to Beau Lane taking no notice of people staring, straining to see who this newcomer was. No doubt they would all be calling tomorrow with some fake excuse, just to find out all about the lad. He stopped Nelly and pointed down the lane.

"That's where the factory is behind that wall. You can enter from the side gate. I live here," he said again, pointing to a house across the road from the lane. "I'll take you directly to Mrs Higgins and you can get settled. Bring your papers and recommendations with you on Monday and I'll have a look at them. We start at six o'clock till six o'clock, six days a week,. All the sixes." He smiled.

"The church is just down that street you can't miss it, just in case you get a yearning to pray." He laughed and winked at William. "Now here we are, lad, hop off and I'll introduce you to Mrs Higgins."

Mrs Higgins was a stout, widow woman in her late sixties; she wore a pinny that covered just one of her large breasts and slippers that were too small for her large feet. She always covered her head with a patterned scarf. She dried her hands on a tea towel before shaking hands with William, eyeing him up and down.

"A bit on the skinny side aren't you, son? Well we'll soon put that right. Mr Shaw, will you come in for a spot of tea?" she said in one breath.

"No thanks, Mrs Higgins; I've still some work left to do. See you Monday, William, "he said as he shook the reins of the cart and called to Nelly, "Move on."

"Come now, William, you must be starving, come to the kitchen, I'll show you your room after tea," she said, waving goodbye and ushering William in and down the hall into a small cosy kitchen.

The smell of food cooking made William's mouth water. "Out the back is a basin you can wash up and I'll have your dinner ready when you're finished," she told him, busying herself at the open fire. By the time William returned, a large plate of bacon and cabbage with mashed potatoes lay on the table waiting for him. "Sit down now, William, and tell me all about yourself," said Mrs Higgins as she settled herself by the fire with a cup of tea.

"Thanks, Mrs Higgins," William said, his eyes as big as saucers. He hadn't seen a meal like this since he'd lived in Mary's Lane and a warm memory flooded back. "Not much to tell, Mrs Higgins. I'm an orphan, I have no one that's why I came here," William said, tucking into his food, savouring every mouthful.

The food danced on his tongue and each taste bud exploded with flavour. William got caught up in the delight of the good food. If this was a sample of things to come, he'd be more than happy to stay here forever. When he looked up, Mrs Higgins was sitting staring at him. William quickly wiped his mouth "Sorry,

Mrs Higgins seems I was hungrier than I thought, it's delicious!" he said.

"Sure, it's just a bit of bacon, nothing special," she said, puffing herself up delighted with the praise.

William suddenly remembered the few pounds the brothers had given him as payment for his work, and reached into his pocket.

"Mrs Higgins, I'd like to pay you for the week now if that's okay?"

"Oh sure, that would be grand, you're right, let's start off on the right foot. Its two pounds a week. That's your food included and I'll throw your wash in with mine. I think that's fair, don't you?" she asked him.

"More than fair, Mrs Higgins, I'm glad for the accommodation."

When William finished his meal, scraping every last bit off the plate, Mrs Higgins stood up. "Come, Billy, I'll show you your room, I've to get to evening mass," she said forgetting to question him more. Billy! Where had she got that from? William wondered. He would soon learn that names were shortened or abbreviated as a matter of course by everybody.

At the back of the house there was a small box room; with a tiny window. There was just enough room for a single bed and a locker. A heavy bedspread covered the bed, with a piss pot discreetly tucked underneath. There was a sheepskin rug on the floor, and a hook on the back of the door to hang your clothes.

"It's not much but it's warm and dry, you should be comfy here," said Mrs Higgins showing him around.

William was delighted; it looked so grand compared to the dormitories at St Joseph's.

"It's grand, thank you, I'll be more than comfy here," replied

William with a smile.

"Well, I'll leave you to get settled and say good night to you." She nodded, then stopped. "Oh, by the way," she said, reaching into her pocket. "Here's the front door key so you can let yourself in and out. Billy, I expect you to keep the room tidy and I don't want to see you coming in here full of alcohol. I won't tolerate a drinker. My blessed husband, God rest him" –she blessed herself as she said this – "never took a drink, only at Christmas," she said firmly.

"I've never even had a drink, Mrs Higgins, so you'll be all right on that score," William reassured her.

"Well then I'll say good night." She nodded, pleased, and left the room.

William fell backward onto the bed. Yes, he would be more than comfy. His own room, his own privacy, good food, what's not to like?

He must have fallen asleep for a whole day, because the next thing he knew Mrs Higgins was calling him for breakfast.

"Billy, its six o'clock, you don't want to be late on your first day, now do you?" she called cheerfully.

"Thanks, brother," a sleepy William replied.

"What?" Mrs Higgins called.

"I'm coming, Mrs Higgins. Thank you," said William, correcting himself.

The night had been full of strange dreams, swirling faces, first his father, then his mother. And then come the brothers with twisted, angry faces. By the look of the bed, he must have spent the night fighting with all his demons.

After a breakfast of bubble and squeak[34], William made his

---

[34]Bubble and Squeak: a dish made of cabbage and potatoes mashed together and fried

way to the boot factory, which in reality was just a large shed. Mr Shaw was waiting for him. He gave him his papers and letter of recommendation. After introducing him to the other men, Mr Shaw took him to one of the work benches, and set William to work. William was more than capable of repairing shoes or making even new ones. The other men chatted as they worked and asked William various questions, but William wasn't ready to tell them everything just yet. He was polite but gave little away. He liked the workshop as the atmosphere was relaxed and friendly and William settled in very well.

Two weeks later, Mr Shaw called him into his office and told William that he had a letter from Brother Mark instructing Mr Shaw that he had been mistaken and that William was not suitable for employment in his shoe factory. William's heart sank. So the brothers had come after him after all. Mr Shaw looked at him and asked, "William is there anything you want to tell me? Did something happen between you and the brothers? I'm at a loss, your recommendation letter was full of praise and now Brother Mark is saying he doesn't recommend you."

William wanted to tell the truth, he wanted to say yes I was rude to Brother Mark. I told him to 'kiss my ass'. In the short period he'd been here, he had come to respect Mr Shaw. He was a fair man. He didn't want to lie. He feared if he told the truth that would be it for him.

So he said, "Myself and Brother Mark didn't really get on and we didn't leave on a good note." Mr Shaw looked unhappy.

"William, I don't know what to do here, they are telling me not to employ you. I like you, you're a nice lad and you seem to have settled in well with the other men. Mrs Higgins speaks highly of you too. But if I don't dismiss you." He paused, taking a deep breath. "Well, they could make life very hard here for some of the men who like you have come from institutions, and even for me, they could make it difficult." He sighed, spreading his arms wide.

"So you see I'm left with a dilemma: do I keep you on, William? Or do we come up with a solution?" William liked his life here in Skerries and he didn't want to leave. All looked lost and William resigned himself that he would be moving on and stood with his head down in disappointment.

"Mr Shaw," he mumbled. "I like it here. I enjoy the work. I like Skerries and I like my accommodation. I don't know what to tell you. If you have to let me go, then I won't hold it against you, sure you have been more than kind to me and I thank you."

Mr Shaw sat thinking for a moment. "William, I've heard stories over the years from various boys about things that happen at St Joseph's and I don't want to judge the brothers. I'm sure they have always had the very best of intentions, sure maybe they haven't always got it right and I don't want to get into the middle of their business. I got this letter two days ago, so I've had some time to think this over. I have come to think in regards to you that if there was no William Le Petit employed here, than what can the brothers say?" Mr Shaw said with a smile.

William was bewildered. He didn't understand what Mr Shaw meant "I don't understand, Mr Shaw, if I'm not employed here, then are you letting me go?" he asked.

Mr Shaw tilted his head, sat back in his seat and said, "William, I try to judge every man by his actions and deeds and I think that you are a good man. So I propose that William Le Petit is not employed here, but Billy Petson is. If you are in agreement, we will change your name to Petson and I will write a letter to Brother Mark to inform him that William Le Petit doesn't work here and sure I wouldn't be lying. If you wish, you can carry on as before. I think you fit in very nicely and I'd be glad to have Billy Petson on my payroll. So what do you say, lad?" He sat back and waited for William to answer.

William being only sixteen did not realise the importance of a name; it is part of your inheritance. Part of your own identity. A legacy passed down from father to son. He knew what Mr Shaw was saying and all he could see in that moment was a way out, a lifeline. He got to stay here and carry on as before. If William Le Petit left and Billy Petson took his place, there would be nothing the brothers could do.

He nodded and smiled. "Yes, sir, that sounds like a plan."

Mr Shaw smiled and leaned forward and shook his hand. "Now get back to work." And with that Billy Petson was born.

Life was slow and mostly uncomplicated; William liked the peace and the community spirit that this place held. On his seventeenth birthday, a few of the men brought him down to the local pub for his first drink. He had to sneak in very quietly when he got home or Mrs Higgins would have skinned him alive. But next morning, she said nothing, cooking him a birthday breakfast of egg and bacon which he devoured, only to puke it all up on his way to church down one of the lanes. From then on, he and a few men went for a couple of drafts every Saturday and Mrs Higgins never berated him for it. Because Billy, in her eyes, could do no wrong. He was more than helpful, carrying water in or chopping wood. He would fetch fresh fish straight from the harbour without even being asked. So Mrs Higgins let the few Guinness on a Saturday slip by and said nothing.

Sunday morning, the men would stand outside of the church, hands in pockets to hear mass. Mrs Higgins always asked the same question every Sunday on his return. "And who was saying the mass this morning, Billy?". Even though she had been to the very same mass. When in reality, she asked just to make sure he had attended mass. William wasn't interested in the mass, or the priest; it all just reminded him of his time at St Joseph's. No matter that they were different orders; they were all the same to him. But for appearances, he went along with everyone else. However, he absolutely refused to kneel in the street when a priest passed by. That was one thing he would never do. He would cross over the street rather than pass them and have to bend his knee. These holy men, who took pleasure at shaming the poor at mass, when they gave what they could ill afford to the collection box that was passed around, always in full view of the serving priest while the wealthy who gnawed at the rail of the altar buying their way into heaven were lifted up and praised for their generosity. No, Billy would not bend to them.

There was also another reason to attend mass. As you passed down the lane, beside the church lived a very cheeky and very pretty young lady, who he found out was Elisabeth[35] Herbert. William had noticed her every Sunday coming to church with her family; she didn't walk, she flounced, and her mother was often seen correcting her. She had thick brown hair and a mischievous attitude. When William had smiled at her one Sunday, she had lifted her head higher and closed her eyes at him and kept walking, only to look back over her shoulder to have another look. William had just laughed it off as the other men nudged him teasingly. He had noticed her, but he wasn't yet ready to let anyone close to him. Not yet anyway.

Sunday afternoons were spent playing Gaelic football with the other men on the green and residents would come to watch

---

[35]The Irish spelling of Elizabeth:. Spelt with an 'S' instead of a 'Z'. to disassociate it from any British monarch.

and judge whether it was a foul or a penalty, causing play to stop while they argued over the rules which seemed to change from week to week.

About a year later, Mr Shaw called him to the office. Shaw's not only made ordinary folk shoes and boots but specialised in making orthopaedic shoes for special customers. "Billy, I have a task for you. I need you to go to Fitzwilliam Square. I have a very good customer there who wants his pair of shoes delivered, and wants them this week. So I'd like you to go to Dublin and deliver them for me. I'll pay your train fare, of course, and I'll give you a few pence so you can get something to eat," Mr Shaw had informed him.

Now William hadn't been back to Dublin since he came to Skerries and his heart thumped in his temples at the thought of returning. *What was there to be afraid of? That was in the past, he would deliver the shoes and come straight back on the next train,* he told himself.

"Is that okay?" Asked Mr Shaw. Who had sat watching him.

"Of course," said William. "That's no problem, I'll be glad to do it for you."

"Now, Billy, this is a very important customer and I don't want anything to go wrong. You deliver the shoes to his house, he has paid me so you need not wait for any note of payment. You can go tomorrow if that suits you."

William nodded. "That's grand so."

Early the next morning, William got the six o'clock boat train to Dublin, his parcel tucked safely under his arm. Being back in Dublin flooded his brain with memories; nothing had changed. Women still sold their goods along the streets, horses and carts still trotted up and down. the tram still hooted its horn for people to move out of its way. He had forgotten just how many people lived here. The noise and the hustle and bustle was unnerving. He'd gotten so used to the quietness of Skerries.

He weaved his way through the crowds making his way to Fitzwilliam Square. Once there, he climbed the stone steps up to the main door to deliver his parcel. A stuffy butler who eyed William suspiciously answered the large door of the Victorian house.

"Wait at the servant's door below," the butler said as he pointed to side steps leading to a lower entrance and shut the door.

He waited outside as the butler had instructed him. On his return, much to William's delight, he was handed a penny tip. With a few pennies in his pocket, he decided he would buy a hot pastry from one of the street women. As he munched away at the pastry, he was so engrossed in his meal that without even thinking, he found himself walking down Capel Street and towards Mary's Lane. He was halfway up the street before he realised where he was. *How did I get here?* He wondered He had no idea.

It was all so familiar, and he was about to turn around and go back when he dragged his eyes to look around him. Nothing had changed; the poverty, the overcrowding, the squalor, the dirt, the raggy children, the noise. Everything was the same. William stood outside fifty-two Mary's Lane with one foot resting on the first step of the tenement building. He stared up at the windows. He was breathing heavily, his heart was pounding. He could feel sweat spreading under his woollen shirt. What did he hope to gain by being here? There was nothing here for him. Women had stopped what they were doing to stare at him, wondering who he was. He turned to go, taking one last look back up at the window, where he had lived with his mother and father. A pain he hadn't felt for a long time grabbed his heart and squeezed it hard; a real physical pain of loneliness filled his very being. He turned around quickly, nearly knocking a woman out of her standing and dropping his pie as he did. But he took no notice and began running.

The woman looked up. Squinting her eyes trying to see who had knocked into her. But all she could see was the back of some young man running as if the devil was at his heels heading back down the lane. Shrugging, Mary bent to retrieve the half-eaten pie, bowed her head and continued up the steps to the tenements. William ran without stopping until he got to Amiens Street Station. Out of breath, he got the next train back to Skerries. No, he would not go back to Mary's Lane, the memories held too much pain for him. He'd finally found a bit of happiness and he was going to hang on to it with both hands.

"You Can Enjoy the Sweet When You've Tasted the Pain", 1885

Every year during spring and summer, there were barn dances held on one of the large farms. The barn was cleaned out and a bandstand was erected from pallets. Hay bales were brought in and placed either side of the barn. One side was for women and the other side for the men. A large wooden table would hold refreshment. No alcohol was allowed as the dance was overseen by the local parish priest. But that never stopped the men from bringing their own, hidden well under their overcoats. William had gone to a few over the years and merrily got drunk, but never danced with any of the young women. Every lady looked forward all year to these dances. It was a chance to get close to a young man that they had their eye on and this could eventually lead to marriage.

This year was like any other year except this year: Miss Elisabeth Herbert was attending along with her younger sister Maryanne and her older brother Patrick. William noticed her right away and she saw him. All the men gathered on one side of the room, the ladies on the opposite side. The men would then have to cross the dance floor and approach a young lady if they wanted to ask her to dance. The parish priest, equipped with a long cane, which he used to measure the space between the couples, circled the room making sure hands were placed exactly where they were supposed to be and a good distance separated them from each other, lest Satan should tempt them.

William watched as one after another the men would approach Elisabeth and she would always refuse, but her sister would take her place and whirled around the dance floor in pure heaven. Every now and then, William noticed Elisabeth staring at him and when he caught her eye, she would turn quickly away. Nearing the end of the dance, Elisabeth could stand it no longer. She motioned to her brother to come to her.

"Paddy, for God's sake, will you get that eejit to come ask me to dance," Elisabeth said through clenched teeth to a bewildered Patrick.

"Who you talking about?" asked Patrick, scratching his head.

"That Billy Petson. Guess he's shy because he's the only one who hasn't asked me to dance tonight," she whispered trying to hide behind Patrick.

"Jayus, you're full of yourself now, aren't you? Well, maybe he doesn't want to dance with you," Patrick had replied, uninterested.

"Listen, if you don't get him to dance with me, I'm telling Da where you were last Sunday," she threatened.

"And where was I? Sure you haven't a clue," sneered Patrick.

"With that Nancy Brannigan from up Milverton way," Elisabeth said with triumph.

"Aw, Bessie, come on now that's not true," he whined back at her.

"Well, Da won't know that, will he? Now gits and asks him before the dance is over, will you?" she said, pushing him away.

So Patrick, not that interested in what Elisabeth wanted, reluctantly went over to Billy and told him his sister would like him to ask her to dance. But he never said which sister and then headed off to ask a very sassy Nancy to dance. William had been watching Elisabeth and knew exactly what game she was playing, so he played along. He crossed the dance floor and headed towards them. Eyes focused straight ahead. When he reached them, he bent close and whispered, "Would you like to dance?" And then he held his hand out to Maryanne.

Elisabeth sat with her mouth pursed as William and Maryanne proceeded to twirl around the dance floor. When the dance was over, William, deciding that Elisabeth had learned her lesson, went over to ask her to dance; only he didn't ask her to dance, instead he just grabbed her by the hand and whirled her round the dance floor, with Elisabeth glaring at him the entire time and William loving the feistiness of her.

When the music came to an end, the men returned to their side of the dance floor and the women to theirs. The parish priest mounted the stage, raising his arms to bless everyone and bid them to, 'Go straight home, no hanging around causing mischief' – he had warned. Everyone met up at the front of the barn. There, Maryanne and a very aggravated Elisabeth stood waiting to make their way home. William joined up with Patrick or Paddy as he was known; who had just been trying to get young Nancy to give him a kiss until her brother showed up and warned him off. The two girls stood leaning on the bicycles they had cycled up on.

"Can you cycle, Billy?" Paddy asked as he took one of the bicycles and gave it to William.

"Well, it wouldn't be my best talent, but I'll give it a go." He laughed.

Paddy lifted Maryanne onto his cross bar. Which only left, a not-too-happy Elisabeth to hop on William's bike. William balanced the bike with one hand and the side of his leg as Elisabeth climbed on, side saddle. They set off with William zigzagging in and out of the lanes precariously and Elisabeth screaming. Paddy and Maryanne giggled and soon they were all laughing as they traveled the lanes on a clear moonlight night.

It so happened that Farmer Foley had a very old donkey that lived in a field near the Golf Club who had a habit of leaving the field to sleep in the lane. William showing off had raced ahead of Patrick and Maryanne, his confidence growing as he cycled along. This part of the lane was lined with trees on either side which made the lane darker and as William cycled around the corner, he suddenly came across farmer Foley's donkey, asleep in the middle of the lane. Having no time to stop, they went crashing into the sleeping donkey sending Elisabeth and him hurling into a nearby ditch. Paddy, who had been coming along behind him, on hearing the braying of the startled donkey and the shouts of Elisabeth and William, quickly pulled the brakes. Both he and Maryanne came to a sudden stop and could do nothing but stand and laugh as William and Elisabeth dragged themselves from the ditch scratched and bruised. Cursing the frightened donkey, William gave him a swift kick to the ass, sending him trotting back into the field.

"You feckin eejit, Billy Petson," shouted a very frayed Elisabeth "This is my best dressed and now it's torn, "she fumed and strutted off at a mighty speed.

"It's not my fault," shouted William "How was I supposed to know the stupid donkey was sleeping in the middle of the road?" he said, storming after her.

Patrick and Maryanne cycled off and left them to have their argument. And argue they did, all the way home until they got to her front door. Turning to William, she said, "You are the most, most, most..."she couldn't find the words. William stood staring at her, waiting for her to finish.

"Annoying person on God's earth, Billy Petson," she finally finished the sentence.

William looked at this young beautiful woman that stood before him with grass hanging from her hair and mud on her face and he liked what he saw. "Elisabeth, I'm truly sorry, I hope that you are all right," he said as he removed a piece of grass from her hair.

"Well, if I am, it won't be because of anything you've done," she said and walked in and slammed the door. William put his hands in his pocket and made his way back to Mrs Higgins thinking about Elisabeth. He wouldn't chase her. She would have to do that. But from what he saw, he was interested.

From that night on, William became part of the Herbert family, spending most of his time in Elisabeth's house as one of them. She even allowed him to call her Bessie as the rest of the family did. The relationship was slow to start with, as William not knowing how to trust wouldn't let his guard down. Elisabeth was a strong, sensible woman and she recognised that William needed time. If time was what he needed, then that's what Elisabeth would give him. So as he became part of the family, she gradually slipped into his heart.

William had an addiction. One that he kept secret from Elisabeth and that wasbare-knuckle fighting. Every Saturday night in the rear of one of the pubs, a contest would be held, with the previous week's winner and a new challenging opponent. William had become very apt at bare-knuckle fighting and had soon grown himself quite a reputation throughout the North County. Although he wasn't very tall or very broad he was quick, as he weaved in and around his opponent. For William, the fight held no malice, it was just a way of releasing some of the pain that he still held on to from the past and strangely it healed him. When he was fighting, fist pounding flesh, blood mixing with sweat and the crowd calling out his name over and over, "Billy, Billy, go on, Billy", and later, his arm would be stretched up high as he was declared the winner, he felt a sense of belonging. He was a person who mattered, someone people admired. In his head, he would say, *Look at me now!, Da! Look at me now!'*

He liked that feeling. Of course, there was also the fact that they had wagered their wages on him winning. So losing wasn't an option. Throw in the purse prize of a guinea and it was a win-win situation. William was careful to avoid Elisabeth after one of these matches as he could be seen sporting a black eye or a cracked rib and he didn't want to explain to her what he had been doing. But like all secrets, they eventually come out.

It was brought to Elisabeth's attention and she confronted him her way. It happened one Sunday as she and William, Patrick and Nancy were strolling along the South Strand. It was a glorious day, hotter than most spring days. Not a breeze, just warm sunshine and blue skies. William and Elisabeth walked on ahead chatting and then out of nowhere, William produced a small package and handed it to Elisabeth. "What's this?" she said surprised.

"It's just a small token. I just wanted to give you something for making me so welcome, so part of the family," an embarrassed William answered.

Elisabeth, surprised at the show of affection, slowly opened up the small package. Inside was a small butterfly brooch with black glass eyes and silver wings. "Oh, Billy, it's beautiful, I couldn't," she gasped.

William shrugged his shoulders "It's just a small gift. You and your family have been so good to me, I just wanted to say thank you," William said looking out to the islands as he spoke.

"Well, surely you should be giving it to me ma? And not spending the whole of your winnings on me," she cleverly injected. William didn't catch on for a moment. Then he turned to her.

"So, you know?" asked William, a little shocked.

"Sure, I've known for a long time," she said as she lowered her gaze and continued. "And it's none of my business. But, Billy, there's no need for secrets between us, I accept you for who you are and hope that you will accept me the way I am. So let's make a pact, let's not keep secrets between us," she said kindly.

William stood for a moment looking down at the sand.

"Elisabeth, it was never my intention to lie to you, it was just something that I had to do, for me. It has helped heal me from some of my past. There are things that you don't know and one day I hope that I'll be able to tell you everything. But for now, just be my friend."

Putting her finger under his chin, she lifted his head up. "I think we are much more than friends; don't you agree?" She laughed.

It was William's turn to smile. He held out the crook of his arm for her to hold on to, and she happily accepted it.

On a sunny afternoon in May, as the waves crashed upon the shore, they strolled happily along the beach, leaving footprints in the sand.

William did eventually get round to asking her to marry him; she had become everything to him: his friend, his confidant, his soul mate and he adored her.

On 17 October 1887, as Elisabeth walked down the aisle, she

noticed that William was sporting a swollen black eye. As she approached and stood beside him, she leaned forward and whispered, "And that's the last black-eye you're to have, Billy."

William, smiling, nodded. "Yes, pet[36]," as he slipped her his winnings, pleasant feeling of belonging spread through him.

William and Elisabeth went on to have three children; Mary, named after William's mother which was mainly due to Bessie's influence. Patrick was named after Elisabeth's brother, and John later known as Jack after his beloved father. William talked about his father and their original name many, many times to his children, keeping his memory alive. For some reason, although William had named his daughter after his mother, he continued to tell people he was an orphan. Only Bessie knew the truth and she would take that secret to her grave.

Later, when they moved to Holmpatrick Terrace [37] in Skerries, William left shoemaking and went to work as a labourer, something he wanted to do for a long time. He felt free, without restrictions. He liked getting the soil under his fingernails, and feeling the sun on his back or the rain, whichever it was.

He continued to mend the children's shoes and that of his neighbours. But that had never been his choice of trade that was the brothers'. Finally, he would do what wanted to do.

William was well-regarded in the community; his love of Gaelic football never left him and he passed this passion on to his young son Jack (John) who in later years would be one of the founding members of the Gaelic football club in Skerries.

On 21 November 1920, William took a very excited Jack and

---

[36]Pet: a form of endearment
[37]Holmpatrick Terrace later named Sherlock Terrace after the murder of Terry Sherlock shot and killed aged twenty-two by the Black and Tans

Patrick to see their first Gaelic match. A charity match held in Croke Park. Dublin V Tipperary.

The Irish Republican Brotherhood's[1] activities had been mounting against the British and the night before the match, key British agents of the establishment had been shot and killed under the orders of Michael Collins (who felt there was no other option left to them as the British Establishment weren't listening to their demands). Unaware of the previous night's killings, ten thousand people crowded into Croke Park to watch the match. After a half hour delay, the first throw-in signalled the start of the match. The crowd were excited, cheering Dublin on. William with Jack on his shoulders was standing right at the back of the stalls, when suddenly, ten minutes into the game, in response to the murders of the night before, the Royal Irish Constabulary and Auxiliary Police stormed into Croke Park Stadium. They coldly opened fire directly into the crowd. Panicked, the crowd started to rush for the exits. William carried Jack under his arm while dragging and holding tightly onto a crying Patrick's hand. He pushed and shoved his way through the mass of people, desperately trying to climb his way out of the park away from the killings. Fourteen people were killed that day including one of the Tipperary players and countless others were injured. This event during the War of Independence only managed to spark more support from the Irish people towards The Irish Republican Brotherhood[38].

William would become secretly involved in helping them, when times called for it. Bessie, a staunch republican, would often pretend to be at the height of childbirth, while IRB members hid under her bed as the house was being searched by

---

[38]Irish Republican Brotherhood: later known as The Irish Republican Army. Headed by Michael Collins, a revolutionary leader

the Black and Tans.

The memory of that fateful day in Croke Park influenced Jack as well. Eager to be a part of this new fledgling nation, he later became a member of the Irish Volunteers in his area.

William was fiercely protective of his little family and would play a big part in his grandchildren's lives as they grew up. His gift of storytelling made him a pleasant companion. He was known to scare "The bejesus" out of all the children on the road with his stories. Just like his father before him, he was cursed by all the women of the road when the children couldn't sleep after one of his story tellings.

William and Elisabeth were married for fifty years, sometimes hard years, sometimes gentle. But always united. She was his rock. The one who held him close late at night when the nightmares came and he was her everything. When Elisabeth passed, William pinned her butterfly brooch to her dress before he buried her and mourned the loss of his best friend. When the time came, he proudly helped carry her up the hill of the graveyard to her resting place. He had made sure as they had gotten older to purchase a grave plot, obsessed with the memory of his father, there would be no pauper's grave for them. Then he whispered, "There was only you, Bessie", as they laid her to rest.

His beloved Bessie was the only person who he had really trusted. He knew he had been blessed to find her and doubly blessed to have so many happy years with her. But still he missed her. However, this time he was not alone in his grief, for he had his children and his grandchildren who adored him, and he had drawn comfort from them.

Home at Last, 12 April 1946

On a beautiful fresh April's day, Billy was taking his usual morning stroll around Skerries, a place he had come to call home, greeting neighbours and other residents he met on his route. He lingered a moment at the harbour, to watch the fishermen in their oilskins and long woollen jumpers. The seals bobbed close to the trawlers with pleading eyes, hoping for a free meal, while hungry seagulls swarmed above their heads. The fishermen worked with great skill and speed, tailing shrimp, for at one pound sterling per ton they couldn't afford to let any of the catch spoil; it had to be sent up to the fish markets in Dublin before evening. He stood watching for a moment, taking in the familiar scene, and then he tipped his forefinger off his cap in greeting to a friend and moved on around the peninsula. The wind caught his breath, his breathing laboured. It was cold and sharp around this part of the peninsula, he immediately regretted having come this way, but the view of the lighthouse and then the three islands made it worth it. Today the sky was so clear, he could see cattle grazing on Colt Island. They would stay there for a few more weeks and then they would be driven into the sea at low tide, to swim back to the mainland, where the grass was sweeter in the fields.

He could see all along the shoreline now, he smiled as he recalled how the farmers queued by the shore, determined to get the best picking site on Shenick Island. There they collected seaweed for fertilising their fields. To anyone watching, it looked like a scene from a western. All poised, as if waiting for the starter gun to go off so they could race to the island in their buckboards. Horses stamped their restless feet, and tossed their manes in anticipation. Waiting and waiting for the tide to go past Peggy's Rock, for then they were off across the beach towards the island. Careful to follow the shingle path and not go close to the sinking sand, where they would get stuck. Women, chancing a lift to the island to pick winkles[39], were bounced about like balls in a bowl. With one hand holding the side of the buckboard for dear life and the other hand clucking their baskets. A chorus of "Holy Mary Mother of God Help us!" and "Sweet Mother of Jesus" was carried in the wind.

Young Liam[40], his grandson, named after him, had done this trip many times. He was to hold the horses, who were very uneasy at being on the island. Being only a slip of a boy himself he found it hard to hold the horses, who could run off at any minute, taking the buckboard with them and had done so in the past, earning Liam a clip around the ear from a cursing farmer. On that occasion they had to leave their task of collecting seaweed and dig the frightened animal and cart out of the soft sand, before the receding tide swallowed them all up. Ellen, Jack's wife, didn't like Liam going to the island, fearing he'd drown in the returning tide. But Liam was a worker and a shilling was a shilling.

Billy admired his daughter-in-law. Originally from the Liberties, she was of Dublin stock and familiar with the tough life of the tenements. Having been raised by her mother and grandparents after her father's early death, she had known hard times. She had settled well into life in a small fishing village with a good understanding for the need of community and unity. She

---

[39]Winkles: small edible snail found on the rocks by the sea
[40]Liam: short for William

had fitted in with ease. She and Jack had come to live with William, after Bessie had died, and had saved him in every way. Losing Bessie had been like losing his soul, for no one knew him the way she had done.

Ellen truly was the salt of the earth[41]. Kind and caring, loved by her family and respected by her neighbours, a lady: always on hand for a birthing or the laying out of the dead. No one was ever turned away from her table; there was always room for one more hungry mouth, even if the larder was lean. TenHolmpatrick terrace or the Cabra[42], as the residents called it, was where the party continued after a rowdy night down at Dwyer's pub, mainly because he himself and young Jack brought everyone back to that small cramped living room to carry on the singing. Ellen was known to get up from her bed, not a drink having passed her lips, and perform the Irish reel or a jaunty jig to everyone's delight. Rebel songs would soon ensue. This would continue well until the early hours or until the drink ran out.

Ellen would still rise at six and light the fire and tend the children. But she had a soft spot for young Liam. Bessie's brother, Patrick had taken the lad up to the bricklayer's union and joined him up. Liam had been very excited: he liked working with his hands building things and standing back to admire his work. He was now two years into his apprenticeship as a bricklayer, attending Bolton Street, and Billy had supported this wholeheartedly.

"A lad needs a trade." Those words rattled in his memory. As if he was looking in the window, he could see the scene, as he was transported back to his childhood home. A small dark room in Mary's Lane. He could see his Uncle Pat standing over his

---

[41]Salt of the earth: a good and honest person
[42]Cabra: throwback to a tenement area in Dublin

mother. The fire was dead, Mary was sitting by it with her hands in her hair, crying.

"I can't lose him." She was sobbing.

"Mary, the lad needs a trade, tis his only chance, he'll gits dat in an industrial school. Ye can't go on like dis, I can't keep ye and the boy. Sure look at him, Mary. Tis not right, anyway tis out of our hands. The court will send him away, Mary, make no mistake about that. Mary, please listen!" With mouth opened, and hands stretched out in desperation, Pat had stared from her to William, who had been sitting on the straw mattress anxious and depressed.

"Why can't ya see dis will work out for the best?" he had cried.

As soon as the memory entered his head, Billy felt a sharp pain in his chest, he tried to shake the memory violently from his mind for the one regret he had in life was not looking for his mother and for taking so long to forgive her for something she had no control over. He knew that now, if only he had known that then. But it was too late, there was no room for regrets for roads not taken. She had long passed and you can never go back.

Turning his gaze to the nearly finished site, Billy sighed at a holiday camp on the Peninsula: *Jayus! What next?* The town had been none too pleased to know that a holiday camp was being built right here at Red Island but then, they hadn't been consulted. Some argued that it would bring employment to the area, others feared the intrusion of their quiet town, as hundreds more visitors descended on them Even if it was only seasonal. There would be no peace until September. As for the young, they couldn't wait, because they had heard there would be a dance hall! No more trudging the four and a half miles to Balbriggan for a dance, sure you were worn out and sweaty by the time you got there. God, then you had to walk home afterwards!

Billy bent his head and carried on down the coastline. His breathing was painful. Ellen had begged him to stay in by the fire, but something inside pushed him to go. He couldn't explain what it was, but he had an urge to see the sky and smell the sea air. It was stronger than his sense of foreboding.

He couldn't give a fiddler's fart whether there was a holiday camp or not, it made no difference to him, but the more visitors there were the more chance of swiping a pair of shoes off the beach while the bathers had their daily swim. They were sure to fit one of the children at home; God knows there were enough of them. He would laugh all the way home at how cunning he'd been when he'd whip up a pair of shoes just left lying on the beach.

"That's stealing, Billy; I'm telling ya, sure as God is in heaven. he seen ya," Ellen would scold him, trying to hide a grin, while she lined the children up to see who the shoes would fit. Billy would watch out of the corner of his eye.

"Well, no point wasting them, now, is there," she'd say putting her head down, busying herself with fitting the shoes to one of the children. Trying not to show how grateful she really was.

Billy took a cut through Hallaghin's lane leading into Strand Street, to escape the biting wind and sat for a moment on a stone wall to recover. He wasn't old, only seventy-eight or was it seventy-nine? he couldn't remember but today he felt a hundred. After catching his breath, he made his way to Dwyer's pub, which was en route to home and something he had taken to doing once he'd retired, mainly to get out of Ellen's way, but also for a chin wag[1] with his mates. He would call in for a small glass of stout before dinner, but today it was out of habit and not pleasure.

He struggled to push the wooden and glass door open, his energy spent. He removed his cap as he entered the dark and smoky bar and made his way to sit with a sigh by the turf fire. Old Dick Dwyer nodded in his direction, while at the same time taking a pint glass from under the counter. Billy halted him.

"Just a half today Dick." Dick nodded, surprised, but complied.

"Cold out there today Billy, for sure."

"Aye," Billy replied and put the 6d on the counter.

As Billy didn't seem to want to talk today, Dick carried on with his work, glancing over now and then.

Goodness, he thought to himself, *Billy looks a little grey around the face today.*

Billy sat lost in thought. The publican's dog who had been laying under the table nearest the turf fire nudged his way closer to him and placed his head on Billy's lap hoping for a pet. When none came he gently pushed his head under the palm of Billy's hand. finally looking down, brown eyes met hazel ones and just for a moment their two souls acknowledged each other. l as Billy sat quietly rubbing the dogs head.

Just lately his thoughts had turned to his Bessie, thinking about her had been too painful before. He had missed her terribly these seven years. No matter that he was lucky not to be alone, a house so crowded it was hard to find time to think, he had still felt alone. He recalled her hearty laugh and he smiled to himself. After all this time, how could he still feel lonely? He missed being one with someone, knowing she had his back and was always there to share his life. She had made life worthwhile. Life had never been the same when she had suddenly passed away. He only waited now to join her. He took a few sips of his Guinness, but he really didn't want it. Placing the glass down on the table, he said his farewells and made for home.

Just as he passed the graveyard, a sharp pain shot down his right arm and across his chest, the pain was searing and it was like nothing he had ever felt before. The pain caused his knees to buckle and he slumped to the ground. Peter Shields who had been coming up behind him saw him fall and ran to help. "Billy! Billy! Are you okay?"

Billy couldn't speak, he couldn't catch his breath, the pain was unbearable, he mouthed, "Get me home", and Peter lifted him up. Placing one arm around his back and holding his elbow he carried him the rest of the way home.

Ellen had met them at the door and directed them to put him in the small room at the back of the house. Billy struggled with the pain, calling for Bessie over and over all through the night. Ellen sent one of the children for the priest; she just knew his time had come and so it was. They all gathered in that tiny room, Ellen and Jack and the children. The priest came and gave him his last rites. Billy drifted in and out of consciousness, calling young Liam to him. He gasped as he asked him to get him a pitcher of Guinness from Dwyer's. "It might just ease the pain, lad," he had whispered.

Liam ran as if the devil himself was chasing him, all the way down to the pub. Gasping, he asked for the Guinness, desperate to be back beside his grandfather. He was barely able to breathe but he kept running, he didn't want to miss a moment with the man who had taught him so much, who'd been there for him, always with wise words. He'd counsel Liam in all things as they planted spuds in the back field. Running in at the door and nearly spilling the pitcher, Liam gently helped his grandfather take a sip, which he did and then he smiled up at Liam and lay down and closed his eyes as life left his body in one long breath.

Whirling through a tunnel of darkness, down, down until he came to a haze of light. It was so bright that he had to hold his arm over his eyes until they could adjust. All the colours were brighter than anything he'd seen before. He stood looking around in wonder when he noticed his beloved Bessie, as beautiful to him as she had always been. Her arms stretched out, smiling, ready to welcome him. They hugged for a long time and then she released him. Standing behind her stood his loving father. Just, as he remembered him happy and healthy. He ran and hugged him tightly, as he had done as a boy. Standing to his father's side waiting for him to join them was Papa John who stepped up to greet him. He felt overwhelmed as a peace he had never experienced before began to fill him. A complete and utter contentment washed over him.

Then from the corner of his eye, he saw her. His mother, smiling shyly, was holding her arms out wide. All the other children; John and Anne, Mary and little Julia gathered around her skirts. He ran without hesitation to join them. They had found each other at long last. Every pain or disappointment, every sorrow or loss was now forgotten. His utopia was complete.

He was home at last.

Mary's Last Known Whereabouts

When I started this journey, I was to find my great grandmother, because I was always told that any records of John Le Petit were burned in the Irish War of Independence 1921, when the customs house in Dublin was occupied and attacked by the Irish Republican Army. Despite my best efforts, Mary was hard to find. But once I found her wedding certificate, it got better and by finding her I found John. After John's death, things got tougher and piecing her years after John and William was near impossible. I do know that on 18 June 1881, Mary entered the workhouse for a short period till 25 July 1881 (records from this period had water damage and were very difficult to read) and she left after a few weeks. With John's death in 1879, Mary would have no financial support. She most definitely would have sold or pawned every item she owned to make ends meet; her teapot, John's coat, plates, the kettle buckets, anything to pay the rent. After that, it would be up to her to find work.

Other families rented a corner of their room to a sub-tenant to help subsidise their rent. Mary may well have rented a corner of a room – taking in sewing or becoming a cleaner. By taking in sewing and mending, she could have got by.

My belief is that Mary's mental health would be so compromised after John's death and then losing William on top of that, I think it is fair to say she would have suffered greatly and with all she had been through, she surely would have found it difficult to manage in daily life.

It should be noted that her brother's real name was John, but so as not to confuse readers I changed it to Patrick. He was a very big part of her life and this is backed up by marriage and christening records showing that John and Mary attended these ceremonies and stood as godparents and witnesses at these events. So it could be that she lived with him for periods of time.

In February 1889, Mary remarried, ten years after John's death, to a man called John Lynch. They both give their address as Dublin Union Workhouse; this implies that they lived there. It could be the case that both were employed as instructors to the young children and adolescents that lived in the workhouse. (Small efforts were made to train them for some sort of employment in the outside world.) For girls, it could be dress making, sewing skills, domestic servant or cooks and for the boys, apprentices in carpentry, stone masonry skills or blacksmiths or shoe makers. I hope this was the case for her and that she found some stability and love.

My great grandfather, William, always claimed to be an orphan and never mentioned his mother or that he had siblings who had died. I only found out about Mary through the newspaper clipping supplied by a lovely genealogist in Glasnevin Cemetery, Dublin, called Lynn Brady. The clipping mentioned at the very end that John Le Petit left a widow and five children (women of that day would never leave out any of their children's births. And would never mention that they were dead. Later, census would separate the column of number of children into living and dead).

On entering an industrial School or any other institution, parents were expected to pay for the upkeep of their children. As if they had the money to do this, for if they did their children would surely not be in these institutions. Failure to pay meant that the parents were denied access to their children. 'Which very much suited religious institutions'. Because this gave them full control over their young charges, with no parents to interfere defend or answer to, they were free to do as they willed. It could well be the case with William. Mary most definitely would not have the money for William's upkeep.

I struggled a lot with the question of why William and his mother never kept in touch. With what William believed himself to be; an orphan, I came to the only logical answer: he had been told his mother was dead, as often happened.

When naming the Christian brothers mentioned in my book, they are fictitious and do not refer to any brother living or dead in that time period. However, the way children were treated in these institutions is well-documented and in this case true.

I searched the census of 1901 and 1911 (there are no surviving full censuses before that) and I could not find Mary. But I know she was alive in 1902 as the document below shows her in Mountjoy Women's Jail as Mary Lynch: arrested for being drunk and disorderly, a serious crime at the time. It is worthy of mention that a note added to her arrest sheets says 'Brother was contacted' and she says she lives in Greek Street, part of the same area she had always lived.

This is where the trail runs cold. I can find no death cert or even records of a burial.

So, readers, I have to leave it up to you. Did she move away and live happily ever after? Or was she found dead in a gutter, another pauper with no name?

Then the search for John's burial site, again I was helped by Lynn Brady and the grounds men of Glasnevin Cemetery. I stood at the spot where the Catholic Church had been taken down; the five oak trees that surrounded the Church still stand today. A spiritual pain hit my chest. I staggered a little and had to sit down. I felt John was with me on this journey and knew he wanted to be remembered.

I was greatly upset on finding John's grave site, learning that he had been buried in a pauper's grave with no headstone to mark his passing through this life or his departure into death. He lay unrecognised along with fifteen other poor souls who lay in the same pauper's grave. So I bought the grave plot and will put a headstone with his and Mary's names on it. So all who passes by will know there had been a John Le Petit and his loving wife Maryanne Douglas.

Now when I visit this spot, I feel peace and contentment, because I know that John is happy to be remembered. I know that now…

He rests in peace.

Mary's Prison Record 1902

Acknowledgements

National archives of Ireland: for their brilliantly kept records of births, deaths and marriages.

To Lynn Brady, Genealogist – Glasnevin Cemetery, Dublin, whose invaluable help set me on the right road. I can't thank her enough.

To Henrietta House Museum, Henrietta St Dublin, who host a wonderful museum showing life as it was in 1800s Dublin. Going there gave me a real sense of what life and conditions were like for the poor of Dublin.

Maree Caffery: Librarian of the Skerries Historical Society. Her research and information was vital to William's story and completed the jigsaw.

A visit to the Jeanie Johnson famine ship, Dublin, gave me a real sense of the desperation and hopelessness of the poor of Ireland at that time.

To Karen Johnson: an archivist of the Congregation Christian Brothers.
en supplied me with William's entry into Artane Industrial School. Documents I thought I'd never find, let alone see. With her help, I finally found William.

To my lovely neighbour Martin Whelan. I can't thank you enough for your encouragement at a time when I was ready to give up. Also special thanks to his gorgeous daughter for her help at such short notice.

Thank you.

And most of all, a special thanks to two very important people in my life, my beautiful daughter Sophie and my wonderful friend Sylvia.."You gave me the confidence to write this story and the courage to see it through." I am eternally grateful.

Special thanks to Fingal County Council, Swords, Co, Dublin. Ireland. Artists Support Council for their kind contribution towards cost of publication. Artist support is very much appreciated.

And, finally, to the people who told me I couldn't.

***"Is feidir liom."* Yes, I can.**